ESUS EVERYWHERE-JESU
ERYWHERE-JESUS EVERY
ERE-JESUS EVERYWHERE
US EVERYWHERE-JESUS E
YWHERE-JESUS EVERYWH
ESUS EVERYWHERE-JESU
EVERYWHERE-JESUS EVE
HERE-JESUS EVERYWHE
ESUS EVERYWHERE-JESU
US EVERYWHERE-JESUS
VERYWHERE-JESUS EVER
ERE-JESUS EVERYWHER
ESUS EVERYWHERE-JESU
ERYWHERE-JESUS EVERY
ESUS EVERYWHERE-JESU

JESUS EVERY-WHERE

KARISS FARRIS

HARVEST HOUSE PUBLISHERS
EUGENE, OREGON

Cover design by Faceout Studio, Jeff Miller

Cover image © MURRIRA / Shutterstock

Interior design by Chad Dougherty

For bulk, special sales, or ministry purchases, please call 1-800-547-8979. Email: Customerservice@hhpbooks.com

This logo is a federally registered trademark of the Hawkins Children's LLC. Harvest House Publishers, Inc., is the exclusive licensee of this trademark.

Jesus Everywhere
Copyright © 2024 by Kariss Farris
Published by Harvest House Publishers
Eugene, Oregon 97408
www.harvesthousepublishers.com

ISBN 978-0-7369-8562-8 (Hardcover)
ISBN 978-0-7369-8563-5 (eBook)

Library of Congress Control Number: 2022945923

Printed in China

23 24 25 26 27 28 29 30 31 / RDS / 10 9 8 7 6 5 4 3 2 1

DEDICATION

To my mother, Chrystal, who tirelessly fine-tuned both my grammar and spiritual compass. Thank you for igniting my love for writing and equipping me to be in the world, but not of it.

CONTENTS

Foreword: Dr. Tony Evans 7
An Invitation 9

PART ONE: KNOWING JESUS IN OUR WEAKNESS

Us Against Us 13
Bump the Lamp 17
Knowing God 21
Starving 25
No More Excuses 29
When You Can't Clean Yourself 33
Snitch 35
Dehydrated 37
Captured 39
Take It Off 41
Idols 43
Main Character Energy 45
A Lifetime of Freedom 47
His Strength Takes Over 51

PART TWO: DISCOVERING OUR IDENTITY IN JESUS

Character Qualities 55
For a Purpose 59
Character Revision 61
Work from the Heart 65

In the Beginning 69
Distractions 71
Imposters 75
Replica 79
A Rich Inheritance 83
The Maker's Direction 87
Doting 89
Nourished 93

PART THREE: MEETING JESUS IN PRAYER AND THE WORD

Relentless 97
Running on Empty 101
True North 103
Keep the Pace 107
Clear and Bright 109
He's Your Person 113
He Can Do It 117
Jumping for Joy 119
Instant Gratification 121
Apart 123

PART FOUR: ENCOUNTERING JESUS IN ONE ANOTHER

Encouragement 129
Love Does 131
Business Interrupted 133
Bridegroom 137
Accountable 139

PART FIVE: DELIGHTING IN OBEDIENCE TO JESUS

Discipline or Bust 143
Repentance 145
Waiting for the Mood to Strike 149
Growing Where Planted 153
Complete Surrender 157
Pain over Pleasure 161
Spiritual Diets 165

PART SIX: JESUS DRAWS US CLOSE

Blessed Persistence 171
Breath 175
Wake Up 177
Not Fully Functional 181
Compromise 183
Choosing Obedience 187
A Guiding Hand 191
Separation Anxiety 195
Stay Close 197
Shifting Focus 199
In the Safest Hands 201
A Place for You 203

FOREWORD

Dr. Tony Evans

Kariss Farris is my oldest grandchild. She is the oldest child of my first-born, Chrystal Evans Hurst. Kariss holds a unique and precious place in my life, as she did in the life of my late wife, Lois Evans. Chrystal had her while in college. To help make life easier for Chrystal, Lois and I stepped in to help raise Kariss. She participated in virtually all of the activities and events of our family life.

My most special time with Kariss was when she would spend Wednesday night at our house after church, and I would take her for donuts on Thursday morning before dropping her off at school. A deep bond developed between us. Lois would take her on shopping sprees and sneak her extra money when her mother wasn't looking. Kariss would even tell us to spank her mother when her mother had to correct her.

As I read through her first full book, *Jesus Everywhere,* I was overwhelmed with joy to see her heart for the Lord and the literary and communication skills demonstrated by the way she expresses her thoughts. Through a combination of personal experience, spiritual perception, and ministry encouragement, Kariss has given us a tool to inspire, challenge, and motivate the reader to prioritize growing closer to the Jesus she has grown to love and decided to follow.

When I read her words, I could only imagine how proud her grandmother in heaven is to see how Kariss has matured as a woman, wife, mother, and lover of her Lord.

It is a blessing to see another member of the Evans clan carrying the message of Christ and using her gifts to encourage others to follow Him. You'll find that reading and absorbing the message of *Jesus Everywhere* will help you to experience Him in everything, in every place, and at every turn in your life.

Thank you, Kariss, for reminding your poppy about how important it is to have *Jesus Everywhere*.

AN INVITATION

In the summer of 2018, I was enjoying vacation with my family when I received a call that my cousin Wynter Pitts had passed away without warning. Nothing could have prepared me for the shock of that call. I had never experienced that kind of loss before. Hearing that God chose to take a healthy young wife of 15 years, a mother of four, a writer, a speaker, and an all-around phenomenal woman shook me to my core. For the first time, my own mortality was evident. Truly, this life isn't promised.

From the stories we heard so many reflect upon after her passing, it was clear Wynter glorified God with her life and even in her death. Though many would say she was "gone too soon," Wynter made the best use of her time by giving it to Jesus. So, with such an incredible example in front of me of a life lived for His glory, even in moments few people saw, I took a magnifying glass to the years I'd lived thus far to discover if my own life would point to Jesus in my passing. But I was disappointed to discover how absent-minded to God I'd been. *Lukewarm* would be the best word to describe myself up to that point. Sometimes hot, at times cold, but mostly lukewarm.

I didn't want to leave behind a legacy of lukewarm Christianity, and in my desperation, I looked for Jesus everywhere. I asked Him to reveal Himself so clearly in my day-to-day life that I couldn't overlook Him, and boy, did He deliver. He was there in every situation, waiting to be noticed in each moment spent with my husband, children, coworkers, friends, and even strangers. Everywhere I looked I saw evidence of Jesus's presence, experienced His teaching in real time, and discovered opportunities to make His name greater.

My only goal in writing this book is to give examples of how I see Jesus everywhere in my own life so that you, too, can see Him everywhere in yours. If you've ever been lukewarm, lived absent-minded of His presence, or failed to take advantage of time not promised, this is for you. I pray that God removes the veil from your eyes so you may see Him clearly and make the choice to follow Him, giving Him the glory in every circumstance with every day of your life.

PART ONE

KNOWING JESUS IN OUR WEAKNESS

US AGAINST US

God called to the Man: "Where are you?" He said, "I heard you in the garden and I was afraid because I was naked. And I hid."

GENESIS 3:9-10

After I put my oldest daughter, Ellie, to bed one evening, she called me back to her room. Even in the dark, something looked awry. When I flicked on the light, I cringed as I spotted a large patch of hair missing from the right side of her head.

I saw no trace of the missing hair or the scissors used to cut it. My husband and I were bewildered. But our daughter stuck to her story: She didn't have any scissors and didn't know what hair we were referring to—although the nearly bald patch on her head said otherwise. After pulling back the covers she had yanked up to her chin, we found the dull scissors she'd stolen from school. And the fist-sized ball of hair? We found that the next day, hidden underneath her bed.

In the following weeks, as I attempted (largely unsuccessfully) to cover up her bald patch, I kept mulling over those scissors. She must have made a great effort to steal them from school in the first place. She didn't have any pockets in her school clothes, so I could only imagine the creativity she'd mustered up to smuggle the scissors home. But that wasn't the end of her deception; once she'd used them to chop off her hair, she'd then tried to conceal the evidence of her actions! She'd thrown her "sin" into a dark corner, but the evidence of it was nevertheless made visible by the patch on her head.

My daughter isn't the first person to try to hide wayward activity. I imagine God in the garden of Eden rolling His eyes at Adam and Eve as they tried to hide their nakedness. And just as God saw Adam and Eve's attempt to hide their nakedness as a sign of their sinful actions, I saw my daughter's hiding under the covers as a result of her guilt. But pretending the mess we've made doesn't exist by hiding it away isn't a solution. The best way forward after botching it with God is not avoidance, not denial, but *confession.*

The aftermath of my daughter's tragic haircut included years of stealthy styling to cover the slow-growing section of hair. But we formed a sweet bond as I crafted adorable looks for her during our late-night haircare sessions. Beauty from ashes, you could call it. To this day, she will barely let me cut a rubber band from her hair without reminding me of her mistake and promising that she will never do it again.

Proverbs 28:13 tells us, "You can whitewash your sins and get by with it; you find mercy by admitting and leaving them." When we admit our sins and leave them behind, God freely gives us compassion and forgiveness. Don't be afraid to pull down the covers and expose your life to God. He can handle it. His mercy will pull you closer, and He'll create beauty where you never thought possible.

READ

Psalm 32:5 ~ Matthew 11:38-30

REFLECT

Look back on a time when you tried to conceal sin, fear, or doubt from God. How did He meet your pain with His grace and truth? How does this demonstrated kindness encourage you to surrender to Him today?

PRAY WITH ME

Lord, I confess that I've so often turned aside from Your way and Your Word, following my desires instead of Your will. Thank You for the light of Your grace overwhelming the darkness of my sin. I recognize my need for You in everything I do. Give me the desire to serve You, and only You.

BUMP THE LAMP

Easy come, easy go, but steady diligence pays off.

PROVERBS 13:11

In the classic live-action/animated 1988 movie *Who Framed Roger Rabbit*, a live actor's head bumps against a lamp. The light swings, casting a wild array of animated shadows over the scene. This visually memorable choice wasn't originally in the movie—but when director Robert Zemeckis saw the first cut, he wrote a simple note to the animators: "Bump the lamp."

The animators pushed back. They explained how much time, effort, and labor it would take to bump the lamp and adjust the lighting. They would have to redraw each frame, add shades to the contours of each face, and cast the appropriate shadows behind them. After considering their explanations, Zemeckis wrote them another note: "BUMP THE LAMP."

If you watch the movie today, that lamp is swinging like crazy! The animators went above and beyond to bump the lamp, adding in shadow and motion that make the impossible combination of live action and animation seem lifelike. And what a reward they received for it! The film won four Academy Awards for its technical skill and innovation.

When I was a college student working at camp during the summers, our camp director would often tell us, "Bump the lamp." In 100-degree heat surrounded by adolescent, too-cool-for-school middle schoolers, this was not an easy feat. *Bumping the lamp* meant waking my campers up with soft praise, back scratches, and worship music instead of a blaring alarm clock. It meant leading them on a leisurely morning walk to the flag where we gathered, rather than a sprint to ensure we weren't late. It meant serving the campers breakfast before I dropped food onto my own plate, making sure they had more than enough.

Today, *bumping the lamp* often means dancing with my kids when I'd rather put them in front of a screen, or cooking a nutritious meal when I'd rather order takeout. Yet I'm always amazed—because whenever I go above and beyond for my family and community, I finish the day with more energy and excitement than I had when the day began.

How often do we give God excuses instead of going all-in with what He's calling us to do? How often do we try to explain away His commands by telling Him about our lack of energy, our overscheduled calendars, and our lack of ability? But God, our Provider, promises to meet us in our inadequacy. When we're empty, He fills us to overflowing so we can praise His name:

> I bless God every chance I get;
> my lungs expand with his praise.
> I live and breathe God;
> if things aren't going well, hear this and be happy...
> God met me more than halfway,
> he freed me from my anxious fears (Psalm 34:1-2, 4).

Here's my challenge to you: Today, bump the lamp. Bring your weakness to God and watch Him go above and beyond as He equips and enables you to serve Him. When you're drained, when you don't feel like caring for your body, when you don't have the patience for that hard conversation, when the limitless energy of your kids wears on you, when your boss's demands feel unreasonable, when your husband isn't giving you a good reason to serve him, bump the lamp...and expand your lungs as they fill with God's praise.

READ

Proverbs 10:4 ~ Proverbs 13:4 ~ 1 Corinthians 15:58

REFLECT

In what area are you most tempted to take shortcuts instead of working diligently and faithfully at the tasks God has given you? Today, commit to "bumping the lamp" in that area, trusting that God will equip you to go above and beyond as you carry out His work!

PRAY WITH ME

Father, I repent of wanting to do things the easy way. In my own power I'm not capable of following Your will. Help me surrender to Your plan and guidance. You are good, You are faithful, and You have created me to do hard things. You have a purpose in mind when I have nothing left to give, so I trust in Your ability to make something amazing out of a life that's submitted to You.

KNOWING GOD

When you come looking for me, you'll find me. Yes, when you get serious about finding me and want it more than anything else, I'll make sure you won't be disappointed.

JEREMIAH 29:13-14

There's a difference between knowing about God and *knowing* God. As someone raised in church, I've known *about* God for as long as I can remember. I've even known *about* Him well enough to use a series of actions I anticipated would bring Him to a reaction in my favor. I'm certainly not proud of that, and looking back at those times, I see self-centeredness—*my* will for *my* life, not His.

While using what I knew about God to get my way, I saw my prayers not being answered. I heard crickets from the Holy Spirit and often felt like I was at a spiritual dead end. Although I was saying and doing all the right things, my heart wasn't centered on *His* will for my life. I believed I knew what I needed, and all He had to do was acquiesce! Getting nowhere in that logic, I looked to the source: God's Word. *There must be something I'm not doing right!* I thought. As I read His Word and prayed, "Lord, what do You want from me?" the still small voice of His Holy Spirit whispered in reply, "A relationship." I might have jumped from my seat!

When we as disciples of Christ transition from performing actions we know God is pleased with to *knowing* God for ourselves, our wills, wants, desires, requests, and disciplines turn upside down. Our minds are renewed from a personal encounter with who God is. Coming to know who God is for ourselves allows us to clearly see His heart and trust His better will. Romans 12:7 instructs us to "be transformed by the renewal of your mind, that by testing you may discern what is the will of God, what is good and acceptable and perfect" (ESV).

My grandfather, Dr. Tony Evans, preached once that we are to look to the Word of God searchingly. Just as a brass mirror must be moved, contorted, and stared at in order for a person to see their reflection, we also must study the Word of God with this kind of attentiveness in order to see ourselves in His Word. In seeking God and finding Him, He reveals us to ourselves with conviction and clarity. Any worldly and selfish imperfection is brought to light, and as we submit ourselves to Christ, He washes it away.

Revelation 2:3-4 says, "I know you are enduring patiently and bearing up for my name's sake, and you have not grown weary. But I have this against you, that you have abandoned the love you had at first" (ESV). God wants a relationship with us, one in which we seek Him, find Him, and are changed because of it. When you seek and find the Father, your life will never be the same (Matthew 22:37; Jeremiah 29:13).

READ

Ephesians 4:23-24 ~ John 14:23 ~ 1 Peter 1:8-9

REFLECT

In your prayer life and in your quiet times with the Father, do you delight yourself in who He is? Or are you simply laying out a list of requests made up of your plans for your life, without a relationship with Him? Have you abandoned the love you had at first when you found your salvation in the Father? Or are you allowing Him to continuously renew your mind as you open your heart for His refinement?

PRAY WITH ME

My ultimate desire is to know You and not just know about You, Father. You are the Author and Creator, and I desire to know who You are and experience You fully. Open my eyes so I can see You clearly as I seek You with all of my heart.

STARVING

I am the Bread of Life. The person who aligns with me hungers no more and thirsts no more, ever. I have told you this explicitly because even though you have seen me in action, you don't really believe me. Every person the Father gives me eventually comes running to me. And once that person is with me, I hold on and don't let go.

JOHN 6:35-37

My husband's and my favorite type of food is Tex-Mex. Every other weekend, we head to the Lupe Tortilla in our city for their perfectly seasoned beef fajitas. The sound of the onions and peppers sizzling on the hot skillet always catches our attention as the waiter brings this delicious entrée to our table—but never until we've already eaten our fill of salty tortilla chips, tangy salsa, and the best doggone queso in Texas. We wholeheartedly enjoy the meal placed before us, paired perfectly with cold Coca-Cola. Once our bellies are almost stuffed, we top off the meal with cinnamon sugar sopapillas, steaming and dripping with honey. Each time we finish this mouthwatering lunch, we push back from the table feeling full to bursting. But only a few hours later, even after a delicious, filling spread, our stomachs grumble again like clockwork. No matter how wonderful or satisfying our last meal was, we humans will always need regular fuel to survive.

When we don't receive the fuel we need, our bellies growl as the body's way of alerting us that something's missing. Hunger is painful and uncomfortable. It can cause us to intake something we wouldn't normally choose just to satisfy a need. And we experience hunger outside of the physical necessity for food.

You may be so starved for love that you date someone who doesn't meet your standards for a good partner—or God's. Or you may so deeply crave acceptance that you start hanging out with friends who pull you down spiritually. What are you starving for? When does your hunger lead you to make compromises? What standards have you lowered, what goals have you neglected, and what bad decisions have you made because you were looking to flawed sources to fill you up?

Despite the heartache and regret we feel after making spiritually unsatisfying choices, the beautiful, redeeming truth of this struggle is that God created our hunger. We were designed to hunger not just physically, but emotionally—and God is the only One who can fill us up and keep us full! If you have been looking to the wrong source for satisfaction, you have been binge eating air. Your hunger will not be satisfied long-term, and you will continue to compromise. But when you and I turn to God after realizing that He alone can fill us up, we are finally able to feel the sweet, lasting sensation of fullness in Him.

READ

Exodus 20:3-6 ~ Psalm 115:4-8 ~ John 6:35

REFLECT

What are you hungry for today? How have you looked to other people, activities, or objects to fill that hunger? How can you redirect your focus to the One who forgives, heals, and redeems you, who "crowns you with love and mercy" to satisfy your longings (Psalm 103:4)?

PRAY WITH ME

Lord, help me hunger only for You. Forgive me for all the times I've compromised, settling for lesser goods and temporary satisfactions. Fill me with the confidence to look only to You for my needs, as the Author and Perfecter of my faith.

NO MORE EXCUSES

Investigate my life, O God, find out everything about me;
Cross-examine and test me, get a clear picture of what I'm about;
See for yourself whether I've done anything wrong—
then guide me on the road to eternal life.

PSALM 139:23-24

In the last few years, I've noticed a huge upsurge in the "big is beautiful" movement. For a while, this mindset was a stumbling block for me—a bandage I used to avoid confronting some behaviors that reflected my internal struggles. I began following social media accounts that showed off curvy, plus-sized women, but over time, I found myself borrowing their self-confidence to justify my own self-indulgence. I was accepting my habitual sin of gluttony when I needed to acknowledge how I used overeating to find comfort in food rather than God.

As a daughter of the King, I should celebrate being made in His image—both by appreciating the unique body He gave me *and* treating that body as a temple that brings Him glory. Instead, I started using the first thing as an excuse not to do the second thing. I stopped fighting the temptation to overeat, then found ways to ignore the side effects of weight gain. I blamed my exhaustion on my kids and my lowered self-esteem on my husband. I glorified my sin so it wouldn't *feel* like sin—and it worked for quite some time.

But the Father does not give up on the hearts of His children. Allowing myself to indulge whenever I wanted didn't make me happier; instead,

I went to sleep every night feeling empty and dissatisfied, uncertain of the cause. I went to God's Word, and the truth struck me:

> Take your everyday, ordinary life—your sleeping, eating, going-to-work, and walking-around life—and place it before God as an offering...Don't become so well-adjusted to your culture that you fit into it without even thinking. Instead, fix your attention on God. You'll be changed from the inside out...Unlike the culture around you, always dragging you down to its level of immaturity, God brings the best out of you, develops well-formed maturity in you (Romans 12:1-2).

I'd relaxed into my culture, embracing a worldview that harmed my body, my relationships, and my self-perception. I asked God to show me my whole self—the lies I'd believed, the temptations I'd given in to, and the truth that I'd used food as an idol instead of turning to God, whom I'd ignored. I was horrified by what I found, yet unendingly grateful. I'll forever boast in my weakness to bring Him glory!

Ask God to open your eyes today. Ask Him to reveal your whole self, and then bring yourself to Him as an offering. The enemy is a master at making sin seem appealing, but true joy can only be found with a renewed mind. Invite God to explore your heart and show you the sin you've closed your eyes to, so you may be fully awake and alive to experience happiness, confidence, and delight as He intended it.

READ

1 John 2:15-17 ~ 1 Corinthians 10:13 ~ 2 Timothy 2:22

REFLECT

What cultural values and worldviews have you allowed to compromise your mindset? When are you most tempted to ignore the truth of God's Word, convincing yourself that whatever feels good isn't sin? What biblical wisdom can help you fight this temptation?

PRAY WITH ME

Lord, I don't want to make excuses. I don't want to compromise. I just want to be all You created me to be. I lay aside the comfort of my sin so I can pick up the truth: that You sent Your Son so I wouldn't have to carry my burden any longer. Father, renew my mind and strength so I will no longer take the easy way out. I want what You have for me, God.

WHEN YOU CAN'T CLEAN YOURSELF

I'll pour pure water over you and scrub you clean. I'll give you a new heart, put a new spirit in you. I'll remove the stone heart from your body and replace it with a heart that's God-willed, not self-willed.

EZEKIEL 36:26-28

Recently, I put my toddler down for her daily nap. Nothing could have prepared me for what I found when I went to retrieve her.

Ellie was standing in her crib, palms up, with brown goop everywhere. She had pooped, stuck her hands in her Pull-Up, and hand-painted her version of Jackson Pollock's *Autumn Rhythm (Number 30)* on her crib as she tried to wipe her hands clean. Now that you have the mental picture, imagine my utter horror. *Gross* doesn't even begin to describe it. Nonetheless, I bathed my daughter, washed her hair, and Cloroxed the mess out of her crib. (Sorry, organic folks—only Clorox could do *that* job.)

Metaphorically speaking, I've done the same thing as Ellie. I've made messes that began with a single poor choice, then created more chaos as I tried to clean myself up. But you can't clean with filthy hands. Why do we, as sinners, keep believing that we're able to clean up our own act? We need someone to step in and lift us up out of our mess. So if you're attempting to purify your own life, do yourself a favor and step back.

Ellie yelled, "MOMMYYY!" when she'd had enough of making matters worse. When are you going to call on the name of Jesus to lift you up and lovingly wash you of your mess?

READ

Psalm 55:22 ~ Psalm 37:5 ~ Psalm 50:15 ~ Jonah 2:2

REFLECT

What messes are you currently sitting in that you need Jesus's help to escape? What would it look like to turn over this crisis to Him? What—if anything—has held you back from calling upon His name for rescue?

PRAY WITH ME

Lord, I have completely dirtied up my life. When I tried to clean it up, I made it worse. I realize now that my dirty hands can't clean anything, and I'm ready to step back and let You take control of my life. Help me move forward from this mess I've created for myself and find cleansing in Your boundless grace.

SNITCH

Don't pick on people, jump on their failures, criticize their faults—unless, of course, you want the same treatment. That critical spirit has a way of boomeranging. It's easy to see a smudge on your neighbor's face and be oblivious to the ugly sneer on your own...Wipe that ugly sneer off your own face, and you might be fit to offer a washcloth to your neighbor.

MATTHEW 7:1-3, 5

My daughter Ellie often snitches on my son, JT, and then attempts to convince me what his punishment should be. I can hear her vengeful tone now as she says through clenched teeth, "Put him in a time-out, Mommy." She gets so captivated by JT's wrongdoing and the punishment she believes should follow that she overlooks the error of her own ways.

When we focus on other people's failings instead of asking God to expose our own hearts, we waste the time and energy we need for personal growth. Attempting to control the actions and consequences of others only results in blindness toward our own transgressions.

As parents, Josh and I want to see our children build each other up and hold one another accountable in love. With this in mind, we implemented a rule around Ellie's tattling. The rule was that if she told on her brother without first attempting to help him or encourage him, she would receive his punishment. Boy, did things change! The tattling decreased, and an incredible sibling bond grew in its place.

God holds each of us responsible for our own behavior. Criticizing others or jumping on other people's failures only highlights our own. Choose instead to encourage, build up, and hold accountable in love when necessary.

READ

Isaiah 53:6 ~ 1 John 1:8 ~ 1 John 4:7-8

REFLECT

Ask God to unveil the sin in your own life so you can focus your energy on changing your own behavior. How can you show kindness and compassion to those you want to criticize? What steps can you take to love those people?

PRAY WITH ME

Father, I bring You glory by encouraging and ministering to others with a heart of compassion, not by gossiping or drawing attention to their failures and faults. Show me how to love those I once persecuted, and give me a desire to build up instead of tear down. Allow me the opportunity to grow in this area of my life. Show me how to love my neighbors!

DEHYDRATED

On the final and climactic day of the Feast, Jesus took his stand. He cried out, "If anyone thirsts, let him come to me and drink. Rivers of living water will brim and spill out of the depths of anyone who believes in me this way, just as the Scripture says."

JOHN 7:37-38

Our first home was the perfect size when we bought it as a family of two adults and one small child. Then we had another child...and another...and soon our home was five-people-full and bursting at the seams. Eventually, God blessed us by providing our dream home—but before we could move, we realized we had to do the hard work of packing, organizing, and decluttering.

Over the years in our first home, we'd hidden things away in drawers, closets, dressers, and bins, and by the "out of sight, out of mind" standard, our rooms appeared clean. But as we started to pack, we were overwhelmed by the amount of clutter we had to confront. We could pretend for a while that the mess wasn't there, but in order to move out of the space we'd outgrown and into something better, we had to consider each item and remove what wasn't necessary anymore. We had no room for junk and disorder in our new space.

When we clutter our lives with unhealthy thoughts, debilitated relationships, bad habits, and beyond, we allow our hearts to quietly store up filth. When we finally take a swig of the Father's living water and are filled with the Holy Spirit, God flushes out everything else. But He doesn't just *adios* our sin and pretend it was never there; instead, He brings our transgressions to light so we can address each one and remove it from our lives alongside Him. Don't be surprised or dismayed when you seek God and He exposes your sins. Instead, feel humbled and grateful that God in His grace examines your innermost being and offers refreshing renewal.

READ

Proverbs 28:13 ~ Romans 3:23 ~ Revelation 21:6

REFLECT

As you've been drinking God's Word, what sins of yours have been exposed? How has understanding your own mistakes and shortcomings helped you grow in your faith and reliance on God?

PRAY WITH ME

Father, I know You are the living water. I desire to replace the sins in my life with the pureness of heart You bring. I ask You to give me the wisdom and strength to choose to drink from Your well alone. When I do, I trust that You will transform me from the inside out.

CAPTURED

Keep vigilant watch over your heart; that's where life starts.

PROVERBS 4:23

On Mother's Day at my aunt's house, someone left the front door open. Josh and I were sitting on a couch facing the front door, and all we could do was watch as a bird swooped in without warning. The bird fluttered about, hitting windows and walls. Finally, it found a perch upon a delicate chandelier. I would testify to the fact that I saw it raise its feathery booty, ready to relieve itself all over the chandelier and dining room table. But just before it had the chance, my uncle rushed in with a pool net, prompting it to fly away.

But the bird wasn't so easily caught. It flew into another part of the house with higher, seemingly unreachable ceilings. The scene was hectic. From my safe corner as a spectator, I watched as three men and a pool net struggled with a tiny but mighty bird until it was caught and released back to nature. All that chaos, just because someone carelessly left a door open.

When we leave the door open to our hearts, uninvited sin will fly right in to wreak havoc. Sin doesn't need a special invite—just an open, unwatched door. And once it's inside, it's not so easily removed. So, we have a choice. We can be spectators in our own lives, sitting back as sin swoops into our lives to cause destruction. Or we can welcome the Father, Son, and Holy Spirit to stand guard over our hearts and use God's Word to take our sins captive before they can run amok in our lives.

READ

1 Peter 5:8 ~ Ephesians 6:10-18

REFLECT

Have you experienced the fallout of a door left unguarded in your heart? Did you unwittingly allow for sin to enter in? What did you learn from this experience? Right now, what doorways in life do you hear God calling you to protect?

PRAY WITH ME

Father, thank You for the spiritual armor You provide to guard me from temptation and wayward influences. Please help me examine my heart and identify the vulnerable areas that need more protection. Put a guard around those places so sin cannot freely enter.

TAKE IT OFF

Do you see what this means—all these pioneers who blazed the way, all these veterans cheering us on? It means we'd better get on with it. Strip down, start running—and never quit! No extra spiritual fat, no parasitic sins.

HEBREWS 12:1

Every night when we get our children ready for their baths, Josie is so excited to step into the bubbly bathwater that she sometimes forgets to take her clothes off. I have to stop her and say, "Wait! Take your shoes off." And then, "Wait! Take your pants off! Oh, and wait! The Pull-Up too!" She is so eager to step into the next best thing that she doesn't realize some items must be removed before she can dive into the place she wants to be.

We have faults in our lives God must remove before we can fully submerge ourselves in His good plans for us. Holding on to sins you are called to release will hinder you from running a good race that brings glory to God. While writing these devotionals, before I knew they would turn into a book, I was eager for God to use me in a big way. I begged Him for a pedestal to shout His name from. While piecing this book together, I realized that in every experience I wrote about, God was teaching me a lesson so He could use me in the next way. He stripped me of the vices I couldn't take to the next place He planned for me.

What aren't you willing to let go of that is keeping you from pursuing Jesus? Take it off! Only then can you fully submerge yourself in the rich, soul-satisfying spiritual life God created you to experience.

READ

Psalm 63:1 ~ Isaiah 1:8 ~ Micah 7:19

REFLECT

What would it look like for you to "strip down" and start running unhindered toward Jesus? What strongholds, stumbling blocks, or lingering sins do you need to allow God to remove before you can more fully experience Him?

PRAY WITH ME

Father, please reveal to me the extra layers in my life that are holding me back—and please give me the strength to release these things to You so I may completely embrace life in Christ.

IDOLS

I've been out of step with you for a long time,
in the wrong since before I was born.
What you're after is truth from the inside out.
Enter me, then; conceive a new, true life.

PSALM 51:5-6

On a scale of God's truth to "living my truth," how difficult is it for you to be honest about your idols? In my own life, "I just love good food!" is the little lie I've told myself to avoid real honesty—which is that I've often eaten to fill a void only God can fill. Food can be an idol for me, and I've often run to it for comfort first, leaving God in second place.

We all have void-fillers we turn to before God. For you, maybe it's shopping, television, social media, or relationships. When we feel empty and unable to get through a hard day, we turn to something we *know* will give us a quick dopamine rush without conviction. We race to a sense of security without doing the hard work of relationship-building with the Father. Perhaps we tell ourselves we're not dependent on those void-fillers, but we're deceiving ourselves—because all too quickly, that dopamine rush can become an idol.

Honesty hurts, and even though it causes only a superficial wound, we never want to inflict it on ourselves. Instead, we cocoon ourselves in the "safety" of our lies. *I don't really need this. I could stop anytime. This doesn't affect any other part of my life*. But God's Word exposes those thoughts for the lies they are.

God doesn't leave us in our voids. He replaces our lies with His truth. He trades our false idols for His perfect holiness. God alone is truth, and His Word is what we should measure ourselves against. Admitting lies and uncovering the idols we've tried to keep secret—even from ourselves—is uncomfortable. But as we surrender the desire to live our truth and instead lean into God's truth, we'll discover the "new, true life" given by Jesus Himself.

READ

Romans 10:11 ~ Philippians 4:19 ~ 1 Timothy 6:17

REFLECT

What are you using to fill a void in your life that can only be truly filled by the Father? What lies have you told yourself to avoid feeling shame? What God-given truths can you use to take the place of these lies?

PRAY WITH ME

Father, please guide me through the unpleasant work of repenting from my sin and surrendering my idols and void-fillers to You. Please give me eyes to see and a heart that's ready to respond with change.

MAIN CHARACTER ENERGY

Everything got started in him and finds its purpose in him. He was there before any of it came into existence and holds it all together right up to this moment.

COLOSSIANS 1:17

Don't we all want to see ourselves through romanticized, rose-colored glasses? A TikTok trend to the tune of "it's giving main character energy" perfectly sums up how we like to think of ourselves: as the main character. Despite what our culture wants us to believe, the truth is that we are not the main characters; God is! He brought us into existence and holds us together. "I am the Vine, you are the branches," Jesus says in John 15. "Separated [from me], you can't produce a thing...But if you make yourselves at home with me and my words are at home in you, you can be sure that whatever you ask will be listened to and acted upon" (verses 5-8). For our lives to make sense, we must understand that it is God—not us—who has earned the leading role.

How many times have we seen someone in the limelight crumble under pressure? How many times have we put someone on a pedestal, only to feel betrayed when we see them for who they really are? We so often crave glory, but we weren't made to take it for ourselves.

Instead, we were made to shine light on the only One who is.

In telling stories about my life, my desire is to share the lessons I've learned about God through my relationships and circumstances. By sharing the mistakes and wins I've experienced, I hope I can encourage you to notice how God is working as the main character in your own life. I'm only a sinner who desperately needs saving, and so are you—but we both share the amazing blessing of playing supporting roles in God's incredible story.

READ

Revelation 4:11 ~ Mark 10:45 ~ Galatians 5:13

REFLECT

What does it look like to make God the main character of your life? In what ways are you playing a supportive role in His incredible story? How can you actively choose—or continue to choose—to serve God by pointing others toward Him?

PRAY WITH ME

Father, please open my eyes to the people around me whom I can serve and point toward You. Please give me the humility to die to myself so I can live instead for You.

A LIFETIME OF FREEDOM

Do not present your members to sin as instruments for unrighteousness, but present yourselves to God as those who have been brought from death to life, and your members to God as instruments for righteousness. For sin will have no dominion over you, since you are not under law but under grace.

ROMANS 6:13-14 ESV

For a period of time, I restricted sugar from my diet to overcome its stronghold as an idol. I thought I was doing well until I was T-boned by a massive headache. My brain and body had gotten so used to regularly consuming what wasn't good for me that my body revolted when the sugar was removed. Though I was making a good choice for my long-term spiritual and physical health, my sugar craving was so powerful that putting it aside felt wrong.

We become so accustomed to—and even dependent on—the pleasures of this world that when we try to detach, the process feels like trying to rip Velcro from itself. In other words, bad habits are hard to break! Indulging mindlessly can cloud our ability to recognize and acknowledge the need to lay down our idols for a holy God. So, it's important to deny yourself at times and fast in the short term in order to experience freedom and spiritual gain in the long term.

Once I had completed my fast from sugar, the clarity of mind and liberating freedom I experienced was worth every minute of the short-term pain.

God says in His Word that sin will not have dominion over us. In spite of the difficulty that laying down an idol may require of us, we can be victorious over strongholds by presenting our bodies as instruments of righteousness instead of instruments of self-indulgence. Recently, I decided to abstain from shopping for a year. Although I had the means to make some impulse purchases, I realized the "high" I experienced from shopping was becoming addictive. I was relying on a new dress to bring me joy instead of the Father.

Maybe you've taken to a habit that is not wrong in and of itself, but in excess, it breeds dependency on something other than the Father. Perhaps you overindulge in social media or television, leaving you with less room in your head or heart for the Lord. Or maybe you occupy your time with busyness so you have no time left with God. Been there, done that! Yes, we will face difficulties when removing or taking a break from the comforts we've come to rely upon, but God's grace and His sweet gift of life and freedom are the rewards for offering ourselves as living sacrifices.

READ

1 Corinthians 10:31

REFLECT

What overindulgence do you need to step away from in your life, regardless of the temporary pain it may cause? Consider what life would look like without being shackled to that time-suck. Would releasing it bring you closer to family? To your community? To God?

PRAY WITH ME

Lord, I need to break from some things in my life that I've become accustomed to—and I know that when I break from them, it will hurt. Help me identify the things and habits that don't make me more like You. Give me the strength to break free.

HIS STRENGTH TAKES OVER

My grace is enough; it's all you need. My strength comes into its own in your weakness.

2 CORINTHIANS 12:9

The birth of my first daughter, Ellie, was no small feat. She was born only after 26 hours of agonizing back labor, which should have terrified me out of ever birthing another child. But, lo and behold, we got pregnant again with our son, JT, and after six hours of labor, he finally showed up earthside.

Childbirth made me feel so weak. I felt hopeless and afraid, panicked and in pain. So, when I learned I was pregnant with our third child, Josie, I was filled with crippling anxiety when thinking of labor. But for the first time, I prayed without ceasing for God's assurance, comfort, strength, and confidence surrounding childbirth. I asked Him to be near and for the Holy Spirit to surround me. I prayed for guidance through contractions and repeated His promises.

Josie arrived after only three intense-but-not-painful hours. The experience had me looking forward to the next time I gave birth. When our fourth child, Roxie, was born, God *really* showed up. He guided me through the entirety of labor, and in two hours, she slipped out with what could only be described as a wonderfully simple, even supernatural birth. A few minutes after she was born, I looked at my husband, Josh, and said, "Let's do this again." Only God's power could do that!

My childbirth experiences have shown me that God uses our weaknesses to reveal His strength with dazzling clarity. The challenge of childbirth never changed, and my weakness was still the same. My focus on God's power in my weakness was the only changed factor. God has the ability to show us how good He is—so merciful and full of grace—by filling the moments we are at our weakest with His glory.

READ

1 Corinthians 4:7 ~ Galatians 2:20 ~ Titus 2:11-13

REFLECT

What areas of weakness in your life can you ask God to fill with His power? How would your life and faith change if you surrendered your weaknesses to Him?

PRAY WITH ME

Father, thank You for Your perfect and sufficient grace. Please give me the courage to turn over my weaknesses and release myself fully to You. Thank You for loving me and giving me the opportunity to bring You glory in my weakness.

PART TWO

DISCOVERING OUR IDENTITY IN JESUS

CHARACTER QUALITIES

I praise you because I am fearfully and wonderfully made; your works are wonderful, I know that full well. My frame was not hidden from you when I was made in the secret place, when I was woven together in the depths of the earth. Your eyes saw my unformed body; all the days ordained for me were written in your book before one of them came to be.

PSALM 139:14-16 NIV

When I worked as a camp counselor for middle schoolers during my summers in college, one thing often brought the counselors to near tears: CQs. Even the letters send a cramp to my fingers. CQ stands for "character qualities." At the end of each week, counselors wrote a paragraph for each of their eight campers affirming the positive character qualities observed in them that week. A panel of handwriting and spelling judges would observe the CQ to make sure they were done in excellence. Those CQs weren't just words on paper; they were life-giving affirmations for the campers to keep forever.

Going through a box of old things one day, I discovered my old CQs and felt tears well up in my eyes as I read the character-affirming words of my own childhood counselors. When my husband and I started dating, we wrote similarly uplifting letters to each other. More tears spilled as I remembered us pouring out our hearts to one another with words of encouragement.

You and I have been written CQs by our heavenly Father. He has carefully breathed life-giving affirmations into Scripture for His children, spoken of how He loves us unconditionally, and shown us His grace. In His Word, we find characters possessing similar qualities to our own and can learn from them how God shows His affection to us as well. Even to those in the Bible who seem unlovable, unforgivable, and unlikable, God shows His kindness. Jesus walked with outcasts such as lepers, tax collectors, and divorcées, and through Jesus, God showed His compassion. When our hearts need the balm of the Father's affection, we should look no further than the living Word of God.

When Josh wrote me letters, I would read them over and over again. Although the words were the same every time I read them, the meaning would change depending on what I needed when I read it. At times a phrase would jump out and inspire me, but the next time I read the same letter, another sentence would stand out and make me feel wanted and loved. In a similar way, God's Word in partnership with the Holy Spirit speaks to us to uplift, encourage, and give life to our circumstance. In the way my husband and I affectionately wrote love letters to one another, God wrote us an entire book. We have to look no further than His Word to find our center in Him.

READ

1 Peter 2:9 ~ 1 John 3:1 ~ 2 Corinthians 5:17

REFLECT

How often do you seek the Word of God to tell you who you are? Find three verses to memorize that affirm who you are in Christ Jesus.

PRAY WITH ME

Father, I thank You for the identity You have given me and for loving me daily. When I can't see myself the way You see me, help me to turn to Your Word. Thank You for the ability to encourage those around me with Your love.

FOR A PURPOSE

In Christ we, though many, form one body, and each member belongs to all the others. We have different gifts, according to the grace given to each of us. If your gift is prophesying, then prophesy in accordance with your faith; if it is serving, then serve; if it is teaching, then teach; if it is to encourage, then give encouragement; if it is giving, then give generously; if it is to lead, do it diligently; if it is to show mercy, do it cheerfully.

ROMANS 12:5-8 NIV

Our son, JT, has a dry sense of humor that keeps us snickering. Our daughter Ellie is expressive with a quick energetic wit that tickles us with giggles. In times when JT's dry humor has taken center stage for us to delight in, Ellie will mimic him hoping to garner the same attention. When that happens, Josh and I encourage Ellie to be herself. We delight in her authenticity because we know exactly how wonderful she is when she is wholly herself.

Like Ellie, I have seen in myself the propensity to mirror another Christian's behavior when it appears they are pleasing the Lord and receiving His favor. But God designed each of us uniquely with a purpose in mind, and when we exchange that uniqueness for sameness, we forfeit the role we were made to fill in the body of Christ.

Holding fast to who God has created you to be as an individual allows you to live out the calling He has set for you. To live out our calling and make use of our gifts for God's purposes, we have to focus our minds and attention fully on Christ. He is able to keep us centered and focused on our specific role in His body.

Don't be so distracted by someone else's gifts, callings, and blessings that you lose who you are. Attempting to copy someone else is wasteful of your own gifts and abilities. Be who you were created to be, and use it for God's glory. Only then will you find yourself in a place of contentment—gaining more than you imagined in the kingdom from the One who delights in His original works, not cheap replicas.

READ

Galatians 6:4-5 ~ 2 Corinthians 10:12

REFLECT

When do you find yourself in the trap of comparison? What does this struggle with comparison reveal about how you see your own identity? What is God's truth about your identity?

PRAY WITH ME

Lord, thank You for choosing me. Thank You for loving me as I am. Thank You for calling me Yours and teaching me how to be secure in who I am. I pray for my brothers and sisters in Christ to whom I often compare myself, and I ask that You would bless them and cause their light to shine even brighter!

CHARACTER REVISION

These have come so that the proven genuineness of your faith—
of greater worth than gold, which perishes even though refined by fire—
may result in praise, glory and honor when Jesus Christ is revealed.

1 PETER 1:7 NIV

One of my constant prayers is asking God to point out my spiritual deficiencies. I ask Him daily to expose where I fall short so He can refine my character and make me more like Him. I don't want to be captivated by culture, debilitated by temptation, or intimidated by the devil.

So, to keep far from these traps, I continually ask God to soften my heart so I can be receptive to refinement.

I've noticed God likes to use my husband to magnify these character flaws I ask to be revealed to me. And although I'd like to say I listen with ease and teachability, I fall short more commonly than not. Often, I want to take on a victim mentality or write off the character defects as "just the way I am." But spiritual growth requires the welcoming of conviction and correction in tough moments.

One day after Josh and I had a hard conversation, he said, "You're self-focused. You don't want to hear about how I feel because you are only focused on your own feelings." After I got over the initial sting and denial, I asked God to mold me. I let what Josh said settle in and realized he had been right. I had only focused on getting my point across, having my needs met, and making sure I felt better. That was a hard reality to sit with—as are most truths. Being confronted with our own sin is never pleasant, but God allows us to better see ourselves. God always gives us a choice. We can dismiss our character defects with a "that's just who I am" statement, or we can choose the hard road of refinement, letting God make us more like Himself.

Through the difficult conversation with my husband, I had to put aside my pride and selfishness to let in godly corrections. Every period of refinement involves a loss of some kind; we must give something up in order to grow. It can hurt to reform bad character traits, and there are no quick fixes for deep-rooted patterns. But I suspect that losing out on a heavenly reward would be far more frustrating than losing a flaw in your character. Seek God's character revisions in your life and allow Him to make you new.

READ

Hebrews 12:5-6 ~ Galatians 6:1 ~ Revelations 3:15-16

REFLECT

Have you become content with the way you are, even though you know God wants more for you? What is God asking you to move out of the way to make more room for Him? Do you have anyone in your life who can guide and correct you? Even though their correction can sting, thank them today.

PRAY WITH ME

Lord, I admit that I've become content with being stagnant, and that I've created excuses for what I lack in character. But I want to change that. Please prepare my heart so I am ready to face my own sin. I no longer want to be okay with excuses. I want to become who You created me to be, not who I've created for myself.

WORK FROM THE HEART

Do your best. Work from the heart for your real Master, for God, confident that you'll get paid in full when you come into your inheritance. Keep in mind always that the ultimate Master you're serving is Christ.

COLOSSIANS 3:23-24

I once had an Uber driver who seemed *heavy*. As soon as I got into the car, I could feel that he was emotionally and spiritually burdened. When I asked him how he was doing, he told me he worked three jobs and this was his last of the night. Three jobs in one day? I felt nudged to dig deeper. "Why do you work so hard?" I asked. "Do you have a need? Are you helping your family?"

"Nah," he replied. "I just like being able to buy nice things." He went on to explain that he simply wanted to be able to go in a store and buy whatever he wanted, whenever he wanted. According to his explanation, that was the sole reason he worked three jobs—so he could *have more.* And although he was succeeding in his goal to live financially unhindered, his worldly desire for material gain had become an emotional and spiritual burden.

Stop for a moment and consider the purpose of *your* work. Most of us work to support our families, pay rent, and get food on the table. These goals are understandable and worthwhile, but now ask the Holy Spirit to search your heart and bring truth to light in this next question. In what you do and in how you do it, are you seeking to make God's name—or your own—great?

As a digital creator, I've struggled with this question before. In a world filled with gifted people, it can be incredibly difficult to exalt Christ rather than our talents.

There was a time when I was working tirelessly for my own gain, but thinking it was for Christ. By God's grace, the Holy Spirit sought my heart and brought my worldly desires to light. I stopped striving for "more" in order to focus on the God of the universe and my role in His plan, however big or small. As I quieted myself to hear God, I felt unglamorous and small at first. Seeing the voices of others being praised made me feel unimportant. But I quickly saw that my voice wasn't ever the one worthy of praise. We were made to make *His* name great—not our own.

Our work becomes meaningful and less burdensome when we ground our pursuits in His purposes. My Uber driver was exhausted working for material possessions. I was drained trying to make a name for myself. Have you ever striven toward a goal that is only beneficial for you, not the Lord? Even unglamorous, unrecognized work—submitting to the routine of a desk job or caring for young kids—can be done for Christ. You can glorify Him no matter what you do for a living.

We all have a role in the body of Christ, and when we arrive in His presence, He will measure us not against our neighbor but by His vision for our lives. Will you be faithful with the gifts He gave you by using them for His glory in whatever you do?

READ

Ephesians 2:10 ~ Matthew 6:19-21 ~ Proverbs 16:3

REFLECT

What do you find yourself working toward in your daily life? What moments or tasks leave you feeling inspired to work for God's glory? Likewise, do you notice occasions when you are working for earthly riches? How can you better position your mindset and actions to work for the Lord and not for yourself or worldly desires?

PRAY WITH ME

Lord, thank You for the opportunity to work toward a purpose in Your kingdom that will last forever. When I am distracted by clout or possessions, remind me that this world is fleeting. Remind me that what I do for You is the only thing that will last.

IN THE BEGINNING

We are God's handiwork, created in Christ Jesus to do good works, which God prepared in advance for us to do.

EPHESIANS 2:10 NIV

As a seamstress, whenever I want to make something, I start by envisioning how I'll finish making that garment. I have the garment's intention cemented in my head, and then I work backward to form the individual pieces. Each pattern piece is carefully designed to work toward the perfect final vision.

God—the ultimate Designer, Creator, and Artisan— always has the end in mind too. He has a vision for an earth inhabited by those who have been made righteous for eternity. His world is fully complete, with all of His purposes coming true. All things are oriented toward this perfect end. He crafts the future, present, and past of our world, expertly stitching it together from the beginning in order to work toward His ultimate goal.

You are a part of His ultimate goal. *You* are a beloved piece of the puzzle. Like a dress being sewn, each pattern piece is purposed for the intended goal of a complete and beautiful garment. In the same way, God wants *you* to be a part of the coming attraction of eternity. You! Don't think for a second you aren't noticed and loved by the Father who created you specifically and carefully for a reason. You were created to contribute to God's ultimate vision by carrying out His purpose for you.

If you're having trouble finding your purpose, glorify God by doing His will and become more like Christ through your obedience. Your desire for Him isn't a pipe dream, and your purpose is not as far-off as you may feel. The Master artfully designed you and gave you everything you need in the beginning to complete what He dreamed up for you in the end.

READ

Romans 1:20 ~ Isaiah 41:4 ~ Revelation 22:13

REFLECT

Whatever the God-gifted desires of your heart may be, how can you work with and use them to bring God glory?

PRAY WITH ME

God, I know that I am Your handiwork, created to do good works that You've prepared in advance for me. Help me to bring You glory wherever I find myself! Give me the vision to see Your will for my life. I surrender my plans for Your plans and ask You to make my next steps toward Your will clear.

DISTRACTIONS

Don't hoard treasure down here where it gets eaten by moths and corroded by rust or—worse!—stolen by burglars. Stockpile treasure in heaven, where it's safe from moth and rust and burglars. It's obvious, isn't it? The place where your treasure is, is the place you will most want to be, and end up being.

MATTHEW 6:19-21

I recently took my daughter to see *Aladdin*, her first "big girl movie." In one scene Aladdin, a thief, is told to walk through a cave holding mounds of treasure without touching anything so he can locate a small, dusty oil lamp. Aladdin ignores the temptations around him to focus only on his assigned task. Unfortunately, Aladdin's monkey, Abu, doesn't resist temptation and touches one of the cave's massive jewels. That disobedience unleashes a judgment of death upon both Abu and Aladdin as everything in the cave begins to melt into lava. When Aladdin and Abu escape, they are stunned to discover that this simple lamp unleashes the greatest treasure imaginable: an all-powerful genie. Distracted by the treasure before him, Abu nearly missed this. His inability to harness self-control and look ahead to the goal of the lamp nearly disqualified him from attaining the cave's most valuable treasure.

The cave we've been called to walk through is life on earth. We have an ultimate goal of seeing God and experiencing a perfect heaven and new earth as our prize, but the enemy has set traps baited with shiny treasures to lure us off the narrow road. Vanity, pride, gluttony, and other forms of self-gratification are just a few of the false jewels the enemy tempts us with to distract us from the true treasure of Christ.

Satan lies in wait for us to be captivated by what feels good despite what we know to be true. When we choose the easy way, we miss out on the experience of God's abundance on earth, as well as the heavenly rewards God has in store for those who honor Him (Matthew 16:27). God designed our souls to be drawn toward Him—the ultimate treasure. Do not be so easily tempted by the lure of worldly gain that does not last. The one true treasure who leads to more life is beyond worthy of our focus and attention. Do not be distracted by the things of this world as we race toward the goal of experiencing fullness in Christ, now and forever.

READ

1 John 2:15-17 ~ Psalm 16:11 ~ Colossians 3:1-2

REFLECT

What shiny yet short-lived treasures have tempted you to take your eyes off Christ? What root desire in your heart causes you to pursue these fleeting rewards? How does Christ perfectly fulfill that root desire? Find and memorize a verse that can remind you of your true treasure in Christ amid the moments when you're tempted to divert your attention elsewhere.

PRAY WITH ME

Father, I want to be focused on You, but this world comes with a wealth of distractions. So many of these distractions can seem like treasure, but I know they are not. I ask that You protect Your presence in my heart whenever my flesh is distracted. Help me keep my eyes set firmly on You.

IMPOSTERS

For such people are false apostles, deceitful workers, masquerading as apostles of Christ. And no wonder, for Satan himself masquerades as an angel of light. It is not surprising, then, if his servants also masquerade as servants of righteousness. Their end will be what their actions deserve.

2 CORINTHIANS 11:13-15 NIV

I walked into an optometrist's office recently and was a little confused by the person who met me at the door. A receptionist sporting a doctor's white lab coat asked what I needed and handed me off to a technician, who—to my confusion—was also in a doctor's coat. I knew these attendants weren't doctors because one of them couldn't have been older than sixteen! Though they wore the uniform of an optometrist and even knew some of the language of optometry, none of them yet had the depth of training, experience, and knowledge that defines an actual optometrist.

Sometimes we choose to model the behaviors of walking closely with Christ although we're still lacking in the experience, knowledge, and pursuit of who He is. In 2019, when I began wholeheartedly seeking God, I was overflowing with the wisdom He awarded me. In that overflow, I told everyone who would listen what I'd learned from His Word. Later on, as life seemed to cave in around me, I lost the fire I'd once had. No longer was I in sync with the Holy Spirit as I'd once been. Even so, I wanted to continue proclaiming His name. I'd come to enjoy the attention it brought. For a short time, although I knew the words from the Spirit were not there, I still expressed His laws and statutes. I quickly discovered I was operating with the spirit of a Pharisee and not the spirit that comes from having the depth of experience, knowledge, and most of all, love from knowing the Father.

Hiding behind spiritual jargon, or the facade of "having it all together," is easy to do. You may have chosen to hide behind "knowing" the right things while hoping others don't notice that you aren't diving deep into God's Word and studying to show yourself approved. But Jesus sees the heart. He walks into the storefront of our lives and knows immediately who is faking it and who has actually done their homework on Him. Let's not be imposter disciples.

Judas also seemed to love Jesus. He followed Him just like the other disciples, yet when the time came to show his love and loyalty, he gave Jesus up for one day's labor in coins. Jesus desires true disciples—those who don't pretend to know Him but instead follow Him, love Him, join with Him in suffering, obey Him, and teach others about Him from their own experience, knowledge, and most of all, love. Only knowing Jesus deeply and intimately can lead us toward the fullest, most authentic versions of discipleship.

READ

John 4:23-24 ~ James 1:22 ~ 1 John 1:6-7

REFLECT

How honest is your relationship with Christ? Are you in true fellowship with the Father, or do you carry the label of "Christian" without investing in the relationship discipleship requires? List the ways in which you feel like you've been "pretending" to be in fellowship with Him. What can you commit to today, tomorrow, and the next day to reunite in a consistent relationship with your Lord and Savior?

PRAY WITH ME

Jesus, thank You for the gift of Your life and the constant and perfect presence of Your Holy Spirit. Although I may have strayed from close fellowship with You, I thank You for not letting me get too far without Your loving hand guiding me home. Your Word says that if I seek You I will find You, so I ask that You reveal Yourself to me as I search for You with all of my heart. Your Word is true, and You keep Your promises, so I thank You in advance for showing Yourself to me!

REPLICA

By no means do I count myself an expert in all of this, but I've got my eye on the goal, where God is beckoning us onward—to Jesus. I'm off and running, and I'm not turning back. So let's keep focused on that goal, those of us who want everything God has for us. If any of you have something else in mind, something less than total commitment, God will clear your blurred vision—you'll see it yet! Now that we're on the right track, let's stay on it.

PHILIPPIANS 3:14-16

When Ellie was three or four, we bought her a play kitchen. I had every intention of putting it together and renovating it into a small version of my own kitchen. But the first time I tried my hand at its construction, I got frustrated by the time and effort involved. Then I got distracted by other things, and the mini kitchen sat in a sad, dark corner, unfinished.

After the unfinished project had been sitting in that corner for a while, my husband, Josh, began gently mentioning it to me. "Hey, Kariss, are you still planning on putting Ellie's kitchen together?" "Babe, show me again how you plan to make Ellie's kitchen look like ours." "You're such a great mom for wanting to create a big girl kitchen for Ellie. When do you think you'll get to that?" His approach was so gentle and loving, I couldn't be upset at him! But he was consistent in his pursuit.

Once I returned to the project, it took days and days of measuring, planning, assembling, hammering, taping, priming, and painting to accomplish the task. Every now and again as I worked, Josh would walk by and exclaim, "Wow! It's looking great! Keep it up!" or "You're so creative. Keep at it, babe." It was indeed hard work bringing Ellie's kitchen into existence, and at times frustrating. But I'll never forget Josh's consistent nudging and encouragement. As I stepped back and admired the completed work with Josh and Ellie, it looked to me like an exact mini replica of my own kitchen—just as I'd wanted. I felt accomplished and fulfilled. Both Josh and Ellie were beaming, and it was a moment I won't forget.

We have a gracious God who is loving, gentle, and encouraging. We can put off our spiritual maturity and drag our feet at being made into His replica, but through the power of the Holy Spirit, He nudges our hearts and gently guides us toward a finished work in Him. Without Him, we'd never be able to get on our feet to push for the prize at all. Even when we grow tired and stray from the hard work of spiritual growth, the Spirit works within us to pull us back to Him.

Keep your eye on the goal of becoming a finished work in Christ. When He calls you, get up and follow Him running—never turning back.

READ

Matthew 6:33 ~ Hebrews 12:1-2 ~ Ephesians 4:14

REFLECT

What goals do you have for your faith? Does God want you to grow in certain areas, yet you have been reluctant to pursue them? What do you need to do to change that? Memorize Philippians 3:14 to remind yourself to press on toward the goal.

PRAY WITH ME

Lord, please open my heart to the areas that need to grow in reliance on You. Please guide me to a deeper faith and inspire my spirit to seek You above all else.

A RICH INHERITANCE

If you're serious about living this new resurrection life with Christ, act *like it. Pursue the things over which Christ presides. Don't shuffle along, eyes to the ground, absorbed with the things right in front of you. Look up, and be alert to what is going on around Christ—that's where the action is. See things from* his *perspective.*

COLOSSIANS 3:1-2

Prior to being transformed by the renewing of my mind through Christ, I would find myself wishing life could be just a little more relaxing. Tending to small children can be tiresome, marriage is often filled with self-sacrifice, the home always seems to untidy itself after just being tidied, and work more often than not feels never-ending. I wished things could be easier, more comfortable. At many points in this stage of life I'd feel numb—emptily shuffling from one task to the next, feeling sluggish and ready for bed again almost as soon as I woke up for the day at its start.

As I struggled with feeling this way, I became blind to so much surrounding me. My small children giggling with one another, playing in our home, giving me hugs with no warning, and yelling at the tops of their voices that they love me. The reward in marriage of having learned to love one another like Christ loves, and the security of our committed relationship. I didn't fully grasp the gift of having a home that was ours, with rooms for each of the kids and extra space to play. I had even turned a blind eye to Josh's and my ability to own a business and be productive with the gifts God gave us.

When you aren't living out a new resurrected life with Christ, things can feel dull and meaningless. Everything feels like it takes so much effort to carry out. But like my grandfather Dr. Tony Evans often says, "If all you see is what you see, you will never see all that there is to be seen."

A side effect of over absorption in your current circumstance is the inability to recognize everything that God is doing in your own life and in the lives of those close to you. Your circumstances may in fact be gloomy and difficult, but God wants you to take your eyes off the ground and look up to Him instead. His purpose for your current circumstances is not to make you feel defeated and heavy-laden. He has come instead to give you rest and abundant life. In order to see all there is to be seen, you must focus instead on Christ Jesus.

When you focus on Jesus instead of the face value of your situation, He will illuminate His purpose for your life within these circumstances. Everything gains meaning—becoming purposeful and filled with the breath of His will.

READ

Philippians 3:10-11 ~ James 1:2-4

REFLECT

What circumstances or current challenges in your life have you been focused on? What in your life might God be using to prepare you for your future in Him? Ask the Holy Spirit to give you a newly resurrected life with Christ so you may see His purpose and live with meaning.

PRAY WITH ME

Lord, when life gets tough and I feel overwhelmed, please give me the endurance, wisdom, and hope to press through these circumstances and draw nearer to You! Please give me an eternal perspective that allows me to see past momentary hardships and look forward to all You have in store for me.

THE MAKER'S DIRECTION

It's in Christ that we find out who we are and what we are living for… part of the overall purpose he is working out in everything and everyone.

EPHESIANS 1:11-12

I love IKEA. Half of the things in my house are from that sweet, sweet store. If you've shopped at IKEA, you already know you have to put the items together yourself. They have these great picture directions that are really easy to follow—as long as you actually follow them. Many times I've attempted to put together furniture from IKEA without the instructions, assuming I can figure it out without them. The result is *always* a hot mess of a disaster. Some items I've purchased have wound up sitting in a corner—unbuilt, unused, and purposeless. How irresponsible of me to think I know better than the maker.

I've been guilty of this in other areas of my life—trying fruitlessly to build myself into what I think I should be without first consulting my Maker. I didn't knit myself together in my mother's womb, nor did I know myself before I was created. So why would I think I could achieve my intended purpose without the Maker's direction? Only the Creator knows the purpose for which He intended each of us. It is our duty as His creations to seek Him in order to find it out. Colossians 1:16 tells us, "Everything, absolutely everything, above and below, visible and invisible… *everything* got started in him and finds its purpose in him."

In Him, we find the answers we seek about what to do with our lives. No matter our age, circumstances, families, careers, location, day-to-day responsibilities, or past choices, we can always seek Him, knowing that He calls us to bring Him glory through our lives.

READ

Isaiah 46:10 ~ Luke 22:42 ~ 1 Peter 4:2

REFLECT

Consider a time when you tried to force your will onto God's plan. What was the result? What desires do you need to part with in order to more fully align your heart to God's will? What desires and goals do you have that God is using or can use for His glory?

PRAY WITH ME

God, thank You for giving us the directions we need to live out the purpose You've given us. Please let my heart be receptive to Your guidance, and prepare me to live out all You want for me.

DOTING

Don't be afraid, I've redeemed you. I've called your name... When you're between a rock and a hard place, it won't be a dead end—Because I am God, your personal God, The Holy of Israel, your Savior. I paid a huge price for you: all of Egypt, with rich Cush and Seba thrown in! That's how much you mean to me! That's how much I love you! I'd sell off the whole world to get you back.

ISAIAH 43:1-4

One time I caught Ellie trying to steal a toy from Target. Though I caught her before she could perform the theft, we had a discussion about it in the car on the way home. I recited Scripture to her about what God says of thieves to help her understand the seriousness of stealing. With tears in her eyes, she began to berate herself, exclaiming, "I try so hard but will never be good enough!" Caught off guard, I said a quick prayer. In God's wisdom I softly replied, "You're right...you won't ever be good enough." I'll never forget the shocked look on her face as she immediately stopped crying and looked at me, wide-eyed.

I continued, "You won't ever be good enough, which is why Christ came and died in your place. He saved you because He loves you deeply, so it's your job to accept His love and do your absolute best to obey Him out of thankfulness." What a moment with my sweet girl.

At times I've berated myself just like Ellie did. I've tortured myself with questions about fulfilling my purpose—wondering if God is pleased with what I'm doing. Am I doing everything with God's glory in mind, or I am self-seeking? I've spent nights tossing and turning, wondering if He'll one day tell me, "Well done, my good and faithful servant." Although these are valid daily questions, they can be heavy when asked constantly of yourself without a true understanding of God's love. The Maker of heaven and earth created us and loves us deeply. When God says He would trade countries for us in Isaiah 43, it reads like a romance novel! I know my husband loves me, but trading a nation for my ransom? *That's* love.

If you are hard on yourself and unforgiving of your flaws, put down your worries. Take a breath and take a minute to bask in the sweet love and grace of our Maker, who leaves the ninety-nine sheep to go after the one—then joyfully puts it on His shoulders and brings it home (Luke 15:4-6). Though we don't deserve grace, He still extends this precious gift lovingly, tenderly, and without shame. You will never be good enough, but Jesus was—and He makes you good enough in the eyes of the Father because of the sacrifice of His life. What a good, good Father we have.

READ

Isaiah 40:28 ~ Psalm 103:1-2 ~ Psalm 64:3-4

REFLECT

God's love is both powerful and personal, stirring within us awe-struck admiration and ardent affection. How do you reciprocate His love? Write out some of God's attributes that inspire your heart to worship and delight in Him.

PRAY WITH ME

Lord, thank You for Your perfect, unyielding love! No words can ever capture its magnitude, and no deed of mine can ever make me worthy of it—yet You have given it to me anyway. Everything You have done in my life reflects how dearly You hold me. When worry overwhelms me, please help me remember that Your love is what sustains me. Thank You, Lord.

NOURISHED

If you grow a healthy tree, you'll pick healthy fruit. If you grow a diseased tree, you'll pick worm-eaten fruit. The fruit tells you about the tree.

MATTHEW 12:33

Like thousands of others during the COVID-19 pandemic, we planted a garden. I kill every living organism I touch (except children), but to my surprise, the children and I managed to grow quite a few things! When the plants were nurtured, watered, and pruned, we saw the evidence of our care and attention in the strawberries, tomatoes, jalapeños, basil, and lettuce our garden produced. The more we tended to this garden, the bigger and juicier the fruit grew and the more we harvested.

But as the world opened back up, we were distracted from our garden and soon lost diligence. Birds came and picked at the fruit we didn't harvest, and the plants' roots slowly dried up, dehydrating the vine as we forgot to water the garden bed. We've since moved from the home where we started that garden, but recently I drove by to see that the garden had been completely overtaken and choked out by weeds.

Spiritual life is as sensitive to how we tend to it as the gardens we grow. When we nourish and care for the health of our relationship with the triune God, we see the evidence of a well-tended root: fruit. Love, joy, peace, patience, kindness, goodness, faithfulness, gentleness, and self-control are the fruits of the spirit. Do you see these overflowing from your life?

When we ignore the work of tending to our spiritual lives to indulge in the pleasures of this world, the fruit we had will be consumed and the roots of our relationship with Christ will wither. And when we neglect our spiritual lives, we stop producing new fruits of the spirit. Sin, like weeds, takes over the place that was once fruitful.

Where are you in the garden of your spiritual life with God? Do you need to cut out the weeds that are choking you? Have your roots in Christ been neglected and need watering? Tend to your spiritual life and produce the healthy, thriving fruit that comes with a God-centered soul.

READ

John 15:2 ~ Psalm 1:3 ~ Colossians 1:10

REFLECT

Consider a person whose spiritual fruits revealed they were walking closely with God. What do the fruits you've been producing reveal about your current walk with Christ? What fruits do you want to see more—or less—of ?

PRAY WITH ME

Dear Lord, please reveal to me what areas of my life need spiritual pruning to yield better fruit. Whether it's my work, my home and family life, or my recreational time, please show me where and how I need to grow in order to better honor You.

PART THREE

MEETING JESUS IN PRAYER AND THE WORD

RELENTLESS

I'm standing my ground, God, shouting for help,
at my prayers every morning, on my knees each daybreak.

PSALM 88:13

During my grandmother's battle with cancer, people all over the world united in prayer. I remember sitting with her as she opened baskets of letters, reading and weeping at the countless pages of prayers people sent after making their request for her healing known to God. Every week I watched as church staff marched around my grandparents' home in prayer for her healing. I listened to hours-long phone calls that my grandparents had with prayer warriors in different time zones. I heard world-renowned pastors pray over her. I'd never seen the body of Christ unite in prayer over one person, and I was hopeful she would be healed.

When she passed away, I was bewildered, quite honestly. I held my breath at the funeral hoping God would do a miracle in front of the thousands of people in attendance and those who watched online. When He did not, my heart was confused. But then my uncle, Jonathan Evans, got up and gave a powerful eulogy. He told of his own struggles, how he had wrestled with God. "If we have victory in Your name, didn't You hear us when we were praying?" he said. But he then explained he'd heard from the Holy Spirit:

> Because of the victory that I have given you, there was always only two answers to your prayers, either she was going to be healed,

> or she was going to be healed. Either she was going to live, or she was going to live. Either she was going to be with family, or she was going to be with family. Either she was going to be well taken care of, or she was going to be well taken care of. Victory belongs to Me!

Whoa.

"This is the confidence we have in approaching God: that if we ask anything according to his will, he hears us. And if we know that he hears us—whatever we ask—we know that we have what we asked of him" (1 John 5:14-15 NIV). When we ask according to His will, it's true that the answer is always yes. Those who have eyes to see and ears to hear understand that we, as children of God, can make our requests known to Him who does not reject our prayers or withhold His love from us and receive a yes according to His will (Psalm 66:20).

But understand that His yes doesn't always look like our expectation. His ways are not our ways. Approach His throne with confidence, knowing He hears you. And then prepare to be in awe of how He may answer, trusting in the perfection of His will.

READ

John 15:2 ~ Psalm 1:3 ~ Colossians 1:10

REFLECT

Think back on prayer requests you've made to God and ask the Holy Spirit to help you discern if they were asked in His will. Are there any prayer requests you've made that you felt were a no, but now with the understanding that you have, were actually answered with a yes?

PRAY WITH ME

Father, give me the confidence in You that when I pray in Your will, You will answer me. Give me eyes to see and ears to hear Your ways, which are not my ways. Help me to see and accept Your yes, even when it doesn't look like my own.

RUNNING ON EMPTY

A thief is only there to steal and kill and destroy. I came so they can have real and eternal life, more and better life than they ever dreamed of.

JOHN 10:10

Recently, I decided to have a cheat meal. I haven't historically made the best choices of fuel for my body, but as I get older, meals that aren't nourishing have much more problematic effects than in years prior. During a recent lunch break, I strayed from a nutrient-rich meal and swerved through Chick-fil-A for a three-count chicken strip meal with a sweet tea, light ice. At the last minute, I tacked on an Oreo shake. But a quarter of the way into the Oreo shake, I started feeling sluggish, sleepy, and sick. Looking back, I now see that I always felt sluggish and sleepy after eating a meal that wasn't good fuel. But since I indulged in these meals way too often, sluggish and sleepy had become my baseline.

Some of us reside in a spiritual state of sluggishness and sleepiness because of the ways we fuel ourselves. But we are so used to living this way, it feels like it is the norm. Life isn't supposed to be lived in a state of lethargy—God offers us so much more! You were created to be fully alive, to experience the joy and freedom that come with life under Christ.

Not only did my body become sluggish and sleepy from my choice of fuel, but I also had a stomachache and a headache. My body protested, forcing me to confront my choices and make better ones. If your life circumstances have grown more difficult because of your choices, take a close look at how you are nourishing your spiritual life. Don't ignore what happens to your mind, spirit, body, or even your community based on the fuel you use to drive your life. Make choices to satisfy the longing of your spirit rather than the desires of the flesh. Only then will you step into the abundant life Christ planned for you.

READ

Psalm 115:4-8 ~ Joshua 24:15

REFLECT

What idols, habits, or strongholds are keeping you from living life abundantly? What would it look like for you to live an abundant life through Christ Jesus? How would your choices look different than they do now? What would your relationship with God look like?

PRAY WITH ME

Thank You, Father, for opening my eyes to the "sleepy and sluggish" state of my world without You at the forefront. You are the light in the darkness, and my life needs to be illuminated. Help me fill my body and heart with only what draws me nearer to You. Set my heart on fire to love the things You love and seek You in everything. I want life more abundant in You!

TRUE NORTH

Jesus Christ is the same yesterday and today and forever.
Do not be carried away by all kinds of strange teachings.

HEBREWS 13:8-9 NIV

I have always been directionally challenged. When I was 17, my dad charged me with directing us home from our church from the passenger seat, a 15-minute route we'd driven hundreds of times over the years. An hour later and in the opposite direction of our house, my dad shook his head in disbelief and exhaustion and brought me home. I wish I could say this was an isolated event, but even at age 30 when asked to drive my grandfather to the home he'd lived in for 40 years from a place I'd been to again and again, I got ridiculously lost when my GPS gave out, all to his hilarious dismay.

At times, especially while driving, I'm easily distracted by my thoughts—so much so that I lose track of where I'm going or where I am, even when I've driven the route many times over. Our walk with Christ is similar in that we can be easily distracted by the teachings and changings of this world, even though Christ Himself is unchanging. As new ideas emerge in our culture, keeping our eyes focused on the unchanging truth of Christ can be difficult. Yet if we do not, we risk being completely lost. But as a follower of Christ, we are not without hope. Just as I can turn to my GPS whenever I find myself confused by my surroundings, Jesus is our true north. All we must do to make sense of the world around us is look to His unchanging Word.

When my husband, Josh, is driving and I think he's made a wrong turn, I don't hesitate to point out his mistake even though I *know* I'm directionally challenged! He often looks at me with a side-eye and continues driving with the knowledge and confidence he is going the right direction and I am the mistaken one. When we're tempted to believe we know the right direction, we ought to remember that our Father is all-knowing and choose instead to trust in Him. In times when our culture-shaped beliefs cause us to question His truth, we ought to look to His Word as the true north. We should continuously look to Him for guidance and truth in a world full of evolving thoughts and opinions because our God is the same today, yesterday, and forever. He will not change, and His Word will also stay the same.

READ

Colossians 2:8 ~ John 14:6 ~ Psalm 86:11

REFLECT

Do you have any beliefs that stand in contradiction to God's Word? What in culture is distracting you from staying focused on Christ? What can you do to reset your internal compass and make sure you're devoted to God's truth and the "true north" of His nature? Find three verses about a belief you've adopted from culture that the Bible is clear on and ask God to mold your heart to His unchanging way.

PRAY WITH ME

Lord, I don't want to be disillusioned by the changing culture of this time. My desire is to hold fast to Your Word and believe only in the truth You have outlined so I can live in Your light all the days of my life. Point out anything in me that rebels against Your Word, and lovingly guide me to the truth.

KEEP THE PACE

You're blessed when you stay on course, walking steadily on the road revealed by God. You're blessed when you follow his directions, doing your best to find him.

PSALM 119:1-2

While attending college at Baylor University, I won the Miss Black and Gold Pageant, a contest hosted by the Alpha Phi Alpha Fraternity where contestants are judged on poise, talent, achievement, and a Q&A session. After winning Miss Black and Gold, the next stage of competition was regionals in Austin, Texas, where they added a swimsuit category. When I heard of this new portion, I decided it was time to begin my fitness journey. If I had to stand on the stage in a swimsuit, I wanted to be lean!

With eight weeks to prepare, I set out to accomplish my fitness goals. My first day running began well. I had a ton of energy, and my form was impeccable—until 15 minutes in, when my whole body started itching. If you've ever been out of shape, you might know exactly what I'm talking about. I suddenly felt drained, irritated, and uncomfortable. I'd hit a wall. Every time the voice on my running app said, "Start running," I felt the urge to walk or slow down. But I knew that if I walked when I needed to run, my body wouldn't learn or improve. My muscles benefited most when they were uncomfortable.

After just a week of running, I felt like I'd pushed through that brick wall. I remember this time in my life vividly because I did the same thing every day: class, work, gym, study, repeat. I was unwavering in my commitment and saw the fruit of that labor. When I took the stage in my sailor-inspired one-piece, I looked toned and felt grateful I had stayed the course.

In our discipleship in Christ, consistency during periods of discomfort leads to growth. Pushing through discomfort creates endurance. As James 1:4 tells us, "Let perseverance finish its work so that you may be mature and complete, not lacking anything" (NIV). Pressing on amid challenges breeds steadfastness. When we follow Christ's direction even as it proves difficult, we strengthen our spiritual muscles and are blessed through our labor.

READ

Romans 5:3-4 ~ James 5:11

REFLECT

Consider a time when God asked you to persevere. What did that feel like in the moment? How did your faith ultimately grow? In what areas of your life today do you feel similarly called to persevere?

PRAY WITH ME

Dear Lord, thank You for giving me the strength I need to carry on in any and every circumstance. Thank You for allowing me to rely on Your limitless power rather than on my own energy. When the going gets tough, please remind me that You are with me, cheering me on to the finish line.

CLEAR AND BRIGHT

We don't yet see things clearly. We're squinting in a fog, peering through a mist. But it won't be long before the weather clears and the sun shines bright! We'll see it all then, see it all as clearly as God sees us, knowing him directly just as he knows us!

1 CORINTHIANS 13:12

For more than a year and a half, I wore the same glasses every day—and during that time, I didn't notice how many scratches and marks the lenses had accrued. I didn't question whether the distorted version of the world I saw was accurate. But when I finally got a new pair of glasses, I slipped those bad boys on and was amazed. Everything was clear and bright! I wished I hadn't spent so much time seeing the world through a clouded filter.

Whether we realize it or not, we see ourselves through the lens of our culture. But this culture has deteriorated, and like me with my old glasses, many of us haven't even noticed. The world has trained us to understand good and desirable things like relationships, success, and happiness through a distorted lens that's only getting more distorted—and often, we forget to ever question this warped perspective. A damaged view has the power to influence how we live our lives: what goals we start chasing, what images we mimic, and even what sins we condone in ourselves. This muddied lens might feel natural because it's what we see daily reflected by the world around us, but like a bad pair of glasses, it exhausts us by putting unwanted strain on our eyes (and hearts). Distorted vision limits our ability to perceive the unblemished beauty of what God created for us to enjoy.

But as worldly perspectives change and keep us running in circles chasing false promises, God's view remains clear and true. It "does not change like shifting shadows" and is not based on feelings, fears, or desires (James 1:17 NIV). God's Word is an exact prescription that leads us to *the* truth, not the popular belief about what's true for right now.

Would you like to see life clearly? Remove the dirty lenses of this world by picking up His book of truth. When we seek God through His Word, we gain eternal perspective that refutes the competing mindset of our day. Once we have found the truth in His Word, we can return to it again and again for an accurate view of ourselves and the world.

Have you picked up your Bible recently? Have you tried on His Word by reading, believing, and acting on what He says? I want you to see what I'm seeing!

READ

Ephesians 4:17-18 ~ 1 Corinthians 14:33 ~ Ephesians 5:15-17

REFLECT

Our hopes for ourselves can reveal how we see the world. On a day-by-day basis, what do your goals, dreams, and priorities look like? Whether it's what you want from your body, your marriage, your family, your career, or your finances, how are these desires influenced by our world? How do they compare to what God wants for you? Are any blemishes in your worldview keeping you from seeing your life as God does?

PRAY WITH ME

Lord, please give me open eyes to see past this culture's confusion and find Your truth. Please inspire my heart with Your unchanging promises and protect the time I dedicate to reading Your Word. Thank You for giving me a guiding truth that endures through the ages.

HE'S YOUR PERSON

God's Spirit is right alongside helping us along. If we don't know how or what to pray, it doesn't matter. He does our praying in and for us, making prayer out of our wordless sighs, our aching groans. He knows us far better than we know ourselves, knows our pregnant condition, and keeps us present before God.

ROMANS 8:26-27

Growing up in church, I was nervous to pray aloud. I'd heard eloquent, thoughtful, powerful prayers from believers with the same gift David had to communicate with God. It was intimidating and often kept me from praying at all.

What does God want from our prayers? I used to think He wanted only our most beautiful, worshipful, and elegant words, but I learned through hardship that prayer can be so much more than that. He wants us to come to Him in all circumstances—to fuss, to vent, to be excited. God desires an intimate relationship—a friendship—with me. Prayer isn't an open mic at a poetry reading; it's talking constantly with your best friend throughout the day and being honest about how you feel, what you need, and what you're grateful for.

In the Bible, those whom God called His friends did all of those things. Whether they were in pain or filled with joy, they let God know their hearts in a way that felt natural to them. We see this in David's prayers throughout the Psalms, as Hannah prayed wordlessly for a child, and when Mary burst forth with praise: "How my spirit rejoices in God my Savior!" (Luke 1:47 NLT). The Bible is rich with the prayers of those who cried out to God whether in anguish or worship, confusion or rejoicing, exhaustion or delight—and in every other emotion.

When you're anxious, pray. When you're frustrated with the slow cashier, pray. When you are grappling with conflicting responsibilities, when you're burned-out by an overburdened calendar, when you don't know how to be present in the way everyone needs, when you are convicted of your sin, or when you are bursting with gratitude—pray. God is indeed for you and not against you! We must approach Him with that knowledge, knowing He is there for us to cast our cares upon.

READ

Psalms 6–9

REFLECT

What different emotions do you see the speaker (David) expressing directly to God? What do these four psalms have in common with one another? What do they reveal about how God wants us to pray?

PRAY WITH ME

Lord, I know You can handle the full spectrum of my emotions. What a blessing! When I feel angry or ashamed or anxious, please let me find refuge from my troubles by drawing near to You. When I feel happy or excited or joyful, please remind me that these good things are from You and that I should turn to You in praise! Thank You for Your unconditional love, which remains steady and unchanging no matter what highs or lows I face.

HE CAN DO IT

Trust God from the bottom of your heart; don't try to figure out everything on your own. Listen for God's voice in everything you do, everywhere you go; he's the one who will keep you on track.

PROVERBS 3:5-6

One time when Ellie was three, she was desperately trying to get her shoes on. It was a disaster. They kept ending up on the wrong feet with the Velcro going every which way, and every time she got upset, she'd yank the shoe off and throw it in frustration. Inevitably, she'd go pick it up and try again. Every time I offered her help, she would scream, "No, I do it!" At the time, it was hilarious. I kept thinking, *If only she'd let me help her, this wouldn't take so long or be so hard. I know exactly how to get her through this.*

Then it hit me: I do this to God all the time. I tell Him "No, I do it!" without realizing that I'm acting like a toddler desperately trying to fit into mismatched shoes. God's wisdom is available for free in His Word! Since we don't have to figure it out on our own, why should we? When I was growing up, my mom would often say, "We can do this the hard way, or the easy way." She meant that I could listen to her and it would go well for me, or I could follow my own teenage devices and find myself lost and confused. Anytime I chose the hard way thinking I knew better, I inevitably found myself in between a rock and a hard place.

Distrust is the root of Ellie's demand to put on her own shoes and my teenage desire to go my own way. Do you distrust your heavenly Father? He is the only One who has all the answers—but He tells us that if we only ask for wisdom, He will give it. And that's a promise! It is up to us to choose to trust that He will keep us on track to fulfill our calling in Him. Seek and you will find that the Creator of the universe has His palms open to you, waiting to guide you and give you the help you need.

READ

James 4:6-7 ~ 2 Timothy 1:7 ~ Psalm 121:1-2

REFLECT

Whether it's stubbornness, pride, fear, doubt, or simply forgetfulness, what keeps you from reaching out to God for help when you're struggling? Whatever this roadblock is, ask God to help you overcome it. If there's an area of your life where you need God's guidance and assistance, ask Him to meet you where you are today.

PRAY WITH ME

Lord, please forgive me for the times in my life when I've tried to forge ahead on my own when I needed to first pause and seek Your help. Thank You for being an active participant in my life and for providing me with the tender care that sustains me. Please remind me to seek You first in all I do.

JUMPING FOR JOY

I'm absolutely convinced that nothing—nothing living or dead, angelic or demonic, today or tomorrow, high or low, thinkable or unthinkable—absolutely nothing *can get between us and God's love because of the way that Jesus our Master has embraced us.*

ROMANS 8:39

From Ellie's first day of school all the way up to the present, she loses her complete mind—in the best way possible—every time we arrive to pick her up. A jumping, laughing, smiley person runs with gusto toward us, exclaiming the delights of the day and expressing her excitement to see us again. Whether we arrive to pick her up early, on time, or late, her joy is unchanging.

In this same way, God joyfully embraces us every time we come to Him. No matter how long it took for us to turn to Him, He welcomes those who are in Christ Jesus without condemnation (Romans 8:1). Yet sometimes we hesitate to face Him. At times, shame that I am late to submit to God's desire for me or His plan for my life has kept me from approaching Him at all. When I know I've put God off, the shame of that knowledge can keep me from coming back to Him even when I feel His tugs on my heart. At points in my life I've sidestepped my Father in heaven because I believed He wouldn't want me to come to Him until I was living uprightly. I've been so burdened by my sin that instead of repenting, I've wallowed in self-loathing.

But *nothing* can keep us from the love of God in Christ Jesus our Lord.

The prodigal son who came late and in disgrace was yet met with exuberance from his father. Our Father will meet us with that same delight. So today, lay down any fear of being met with condemnation, shame, accusations, or frustrations when you call out for God. Nothing will separate you from His love!

READ

Ephesians 6:11 ~ Psalm 73:28 ~ Isaiah 55:6

REFLECT

Consider a time when the enemy tricked you into believing that God wouldn't receive you because of your past mistakes. How did God's love and grace disprove this lie? Today, how does this experience prepare you to run back to your Father, who has been waiting for you all along?

PRAY WITH ME

Lord, I'm sorry for not coming to You sooner. I fell into the enemy's trap of believing that You'd meet me with accusations and disappointment. But I know now that You just want me to come home to You, and I'm ready to run into Your loving arms.

INSTANT GRATIFICATION

Wait for the Lord; be strong, and let your heart take courage; wait for the Lord!

PSALM 27:14 ESV

In an age that values instant gratification, waiting is a lost art. With the tiny devices we keep in our pockets, we can share our thoughts with the world almost as quickly as we can think them. We can order a week's worth of groceries and find them on our porch in an hour, and we can pull up Netflix or *Candy Crush* to keep us entertained the second we find ourselves bored. Getting what we want as soon as we've thought to want it is now an expectation.

But, my friends, even in the age of Amazon Prime, God is not our Alexa. He doesn't grant our prayers in an instant with the mechanical answer of "Yes, child, I've added that to your prayer request cart." So how do we respond when He answers in His own time? How do we cope with having to wait?

Sometimes we assume God doesn't hear us when we don't receive the answer we are looking for in an American minute. Our response can be to lose faith and interest in Him, or to grumble and complain. When the world around us is so quick to deliver, we find it frustrating when God doesn't appease us with the instant gratification to which we've grown accustomed.

But understand this: God is constant, not instant. His time is not ours, and His ways we can't understand (Isaiah 55:8-9). When you're in the thick of it, He hears, He understands, and He has His best in store for you in His own time—which may or may not align with your expectation. Pray for the patience you need to wait for the perfect timing of the Master Planner.

READ

James 5:7-8 ~ Romans 12:12 ~ Psalm 145:18-19

REFLECT

So many of us are guilty of viewing God as our spiritual Alexa—a machine ready with a quick answer to satisfy us. If this is you, how do you need to change your view of God? How can you respond in faith when God's answers to your prayers are different from what you asked Him for?

PRAY WITH ME

Lord, I'm sorry for treating You like a genie in a bottle. I've put You on the back burner and only came to You when I needed something. I want to change that. Help me take the steps needed to mold our relationship into what it's supposed to be: a Father and His child.

APART

Anyone who intends to come with me has to let me lead. You're not in the driver's seat; I am. Don't run from suffering; embrace it. Follow me and I'll show you how. Self-help is no help at all. Self-sacrifice is the way, my way, to saving yourself, your true self. What good would it do to get everything you want and lose you, the real you? What could you ever trade your soul for?

MARK 8:34-37

The Bible can free you if you grasp it with faith, but it can also trouble your heart with conviction when you take its commands seriously. Once we read what it truly says—rather than what we want it to say—the Word calls us out, tells us when we're wrong, and gives us instructions for how we need to change. Jesus welcomed everyone, but He also called everyone in sin to repent. "Neither do I condemn you; go, and from now on sin no more," Jesus said to the woman at the well who was living with a man who wasn't her husband (John 8:11 ESV). Reading the Word of God has caused me to cringe physically when His words didn't line up with my vision of Him. Our strong opposing reactions to Scripture reveal the tension between our sinful natures and God's perfect Word. The ungodliness inside of us rejects the truth.

Jesus's words were radical when He said them. Crowds followed Him for this reason, and many abhorred Him for the same reason. Today, following Jesus can feel even more radical. But God's Word has not changed, and we must adjust our views for His, not the other way around. To follow Jesus and obey God's unchanging commands will look radical against a wayward culture, but Christ has called us to obey Him and be a set-apart people. "I am holy; you be holy" (1 Peter 1:16). That call should inspire reverence and even fear.

Being set apart requires us to kill our fleshly desires daily. That's tough to do! But the gain on the other side of the pain is a life lived for the glory of a God who is good and fair and shows us grace unending no matter how many times we fail.

READ

Matthew 6:24 ~ Galatians 1:10

REFLECT

In which areas of your life do you feel like you're riding the fence between honoring God and submitting to culture? What do you need to change in order to commit your heart, mind, and soul completely and exclusively to God? What's one small change you can make for the next week to better devote your heart to seeing God as He really is?

PRAY WITH ME

Lord, give me the courage and strength I need to live a life dedicated to following You. Take away the desires and distractions that cause me to take my eyes off the path You've set before me. Mold my heart to crave You above all else. Thank You for giving me a life filled with purpose where I have the privilege of worshiping at the throne of the almighty King.

PART FOUR

ENCOUNTERING JESUS IN ONE ANOTHER

ENCOURAGEMENT

Therefore, my beloved brothers, be steadfast, immovable, always abounding in the work of the Lord, knowing that in the Lord your labor is not in vain.

1 CORINTHIANS 15:58

Honoring my body as a temple of the Holy Spirit has been a struggle for me over the years. I've hit walls during the journey and even wanted to give up on a healthy lifestyle altogether. One day as I grabbed my keys to drive to a fast-food restaurant I knew wasn't the best for me, flowers arrived at my doorstep. My husband had noticed my discouragement and took it upon himself to provide comfort and strength in the form of flowers and an encouraging note.

Instead of falling into the familiar trap of hopelessness and making a beeline for hot fries, I read the note aloud over and over: "Let's not allow ourselves to get fatigued doing good. At the right time we will harvest a good crop if we don't give up, or quit" (Galatians 6:9). A small gesture of encouragement rerouted my trajectory of self-sabotage. Instead of eating fast food shamefully in my car, I was rejoicing in the truth of God's Word and the fullness it provides. And all it took was a short note to remind me.

Today, intentionally encourage someone. Let them know that you see them, that you understand their struggle, that you're so proud of how far they've come, and that you're inspired by the way God's working in their life! You don't know the difference it could make in their decisions today.

READ

Hebrews 10:24-25 ~ 1 Thessalonians 5:11 ~ 1 Peter 1:22

REFLECT

What can you do today to encourage someone in your circle? Is someone you know struggling, someone who could use an uplifting note or gift? And what about you? Do you find yourself losing strength when something gets difficult, to the point of neglecting your standards? What is the end result of *not* giving in to momentary satisfaction? Let this be your motivation!

PRAY WITH ME

Father, thank You for putting me in a position to encourage others. Point out someone whom I can encourage today. Point out the weak, tired, oppressed, and hungry, and equip me to energize them through the gift of Your Holy Spirit.

LOVE DOES

Love is patient and kind; love does not envy or boast; it is not arrogant or rude. It does not insist on its own way; it is not irritable or resentful; it does not rejoice at wrongdoing, but rejoices with the truth. Love bears all things, believes all things, hopes all things, endures all things.

1 CORINTHIANS 13:4-7 ESV

When I was in junior high, I told a lie to my best friend, Aaqila. I don't remember the lie itself, but she found out. She would have been justified in saying, "You know what, I have to weed out people in my life who aren't good for me." But instead, she pulled me aside as a mature sixth grader and said, "I know you lied, and it's not okay. Truth is what God has asked of us. If you continue to walk down this path, we can't be as close." She approached me lovingly, told me what God expects of me, and set a personal boundary. That is love.

I remember that conversation to this day because *that's* the community God wants for us. That's what loving your neighbor as yourself looks like, and it convicted me to change. We live in a "cut the toxicity out of your life" culture. And though there is a time for setting boundaries with others, the enemy has done a number on us—deceiving us into believing we are to be our own number-one priority. But God did not call us to love ourselves. He called us to love others *like* we love ourselves. Loving ourselves comes naturally. Christ instead called us to do what's harder by loving our family, our neighbors, and yes, even our enemies.

Don't let the enemy fool you into thinking you're supposed to put yourself first over everything and everyone. It feels unnatural to put others above yourself. Our flesh is weak and lives in opposition to God's Word, so we must check our feelings against His truth, especially in our relationships with others. We don't always need new friends; often, we just need to learn to better love the ones we have. We can do this by being patient and kind, avoiding envying or boasting, not keeping record of wrongdoings, and yes, sometimes enduring a difficult relationship for the purpose of bringing God glory with our love.

READ

Colossians 3:13 ~ Luke 6:35 ~ Matthew 6:14-15

REFLECT

How can you strengthen the relationships around you by caring for others more than you care for yourself ? Have you been tempted to cut someone out when God is instead calling you to love? Is there someone who has hurt you that you need to forgive?

PRAY WITH ME

Father, forgive me for any unforgiveness in my heart. Point out how I can better love and serve the people around me. Search my heart and expose in me the selfish desires that keep me from loving those around me.

BUSINESS INTERRUPTED

*Be quick to give a meal to the hungry, a bed to the homeless—cheerfully. Be generous with the different things God gave you, passing them around so all get in on it: if words, let it be God's words; if help, let it be God's hearty help. That way, God's bright presence will be evident in everything through Jesus, and **he'll** get all the credit as the One mighty in everything.*

1 PETER 4:10-11

A woman stopped me one day while I was walking through Target and began telling me her story. Her husband left, her bills were due, and her apartment complex fined her. She had a job, she was responsible, but she needed a little extra help. I told her if I helped her, she had to let me pray for her. So in the middle of Target, I put a hand on her shoulder and we cried out to God. Then I did what I could to help. I far from performed a miracle for her finances, but I did allow myself to be interrupted in order to give God the glory.

Everywhere He went, Jesus was approached and interrupted with requests for miracles—and judging by what the gospels describe, Jesus performed those miracles about as often as He was asked for them. The woman with the issue of blood stopped Him while He was walking with the disciples in a crowd (Luke 8:43-45). The centurion asked Jesus to heal his ailing servant as soon as Jesus entered Capernaum (Luke 7:1-10). Another sick man was literally lowered through a roof while Jesus was teaching (Luke 5:17-39). Yet we never see Jesus say, "Um, I'm actually in the middle of something right now. Can you come back tomorrow?" He didn't see interruptions as diversions but rather as opportunities to serve.

In Philippians 2:4 we're told, "Put yourself aside, and help others get ahead. Don't be obsessed with getting your own advantage. Forget yourselves long enough to lend a helping hand." How many times have we missed opportunities to bless people because we've closed ourselves off to interruptions? We ask Jesus to use us, but are we really ready when He sends disruptions into the flow of our day? To serve Jesus, we must be willing to be interrupted like He was. Serving Jesus means serving others—anytime.

READ

Micah 6:8 ~ Isaiah 30:21

REFLECT

What distractions are keeping you from listening when the gentle voice of the Lord nudges you to do something? Next time you are interrupted by someone in need, how can you lay yourself aside to lend a helping hand and experience the true humility of Jesus?

PRAY WITH ME

Lord, I apologize for my focus being on things other than You. Your voice is all I want to hear. Help all other things fade away. Use me in big ways, Father, so Your kingdom will come and Your will would be done! I don't want to miss a beat with You. I surrender all of my selfishness and pride!

BRIDEGROOM

Can anything ever separate us from Christ's love? Does it mean he no longer loves us if we have trouble or calamity, or are persecuted, or hungry, or destitute, or in danger, or threatened with death?... No, despite all these things, overwhelming victory is ours through Christ, who loved us.

ROMANS 8:35, 37 NLT

A while ago, Josh and I were on a date night when I asked him if he would change anything about me. I'm not going to lie; the question was a trap. Face, meet palm. As I waited for him to say something about my appearance or point out a character flaw, I was poised to pounce. Yet he surprised me and said, "I would want you to know how much I love you."

Josh knows I'm a sucker for a romantic comedy, so at first I thought he was just trying to play into my fantasy world of perfect answers! But as I let the answer soak in, I realized that when I gave him the opportunity to perform a deep dive on my flaws, he wanted instead to increase my understanding of his love for me.

God's love for us is the same. It takes precedence over our shortcomings. Although He teaches us and holds us accountable for our actions, He makes known His unending love for us as His bride above all else. He is a God who judges, but He is also a God of love. If your sight becomes obstructed by your imperfections, know that God's deepest desire for you is to know Him and be loved by Him. He's the ultimate bridegroom.

READ

Jeremiah 31:3 ~ Deuteronomy 7:9 ~ Ephesians 2:4-5

REFLECT

What keeps you from acknowledging and accepting the love God has for you? Today, write down a Bible verse that reminds you of God's deep, never-ending affection for you. Put it somewhere you'll see it often, and remember it throughout the day.

PRAY WITH ME

Dear God, thank You for Your unwavering and unconditional love. Even when my love falters and my attention is drawn away from You, You remain faithful in Your promises to me. Please help me to accept and cherish Your perfect love for my imperfect soul. Let this love inspire worship within me, and lead me to opportunities to love those around me in the same way.

ACCOUNTABLE

It's better to have a partner than go it alone.
Share the work, share the wealth.
And if one falls down, the other helps.

ECCLESIASTES 4:9-10

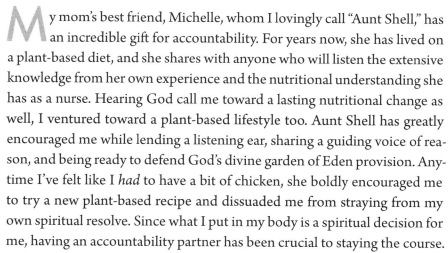

My mom's best friend, Michelle, whom I lovingly call "Aunt Shell," has an incredible gift for accountability. For years now, she has lived on a plant-based diet, and she shares with anyone who will listen the extensive knowledge from her own experience and the nutritional understanding she has as a nurse. Hearing God call me toward a lasting nutritional change as well, I ventured toward a plant-based lifestyle too. Aunt Shell has greatly encouraged me while lending a listening ear, sharing a guiding voice of reason, and being ready to defend God's divine garden of Eden provision. Anytime I've felt like I *had* to have a bit of chicken, she boldly encouraged me to try a new plant-based recipe and dissuaded me from straying from my own spiritual resolve. Since what I put in my body is a spiritual decision for me, having an accountability partner has been crucial to staying the course.

Accountability is spiritual supervision. When we struggle in an area of our lives, it's crucial to seek out a mature disciple of Christ and walk with them as we learn to fall in step. Accountability is a clear, audible voice checking us against the Word of God and our own decisions in real time. Hearing a person close to you repeating a biblical truth you've been running from or sinning against is *hard*, but necessary. Iron sharpens iron. Note that whenever the enemy taunted Jesus, Jesus was alone.

When seeking out spiritual accountability, search for someone who loves you but loves God more. We must seek the truth in order for true accountability to occur. Then, when accountability partners hold something to the light in front of us, we must be honest about the messes they show us.

READ

Romans 1:18-27

REFLECT

Have you suppressed the truth in any area of your life in order to live in the way you please? Sit with these verses and ask the Holy Spirit to reveal through His Word any foolishness in your life. Is there someone close to you who can hold you accountable, in love, using God's Word?

PRAY WITH ME

Father, do not give me over to a debased mind. Continue to convict me and show me the areas in my life that need to be refined for Your glory. Place someone in my life to be an accountability partner. Lavish wisdom on them so they can help bring Your truth to light for me.

PART FIVE

DELIGHTING IN OBEDIENCE TO JESUS

DISCIPLINE OR BUST

This trouble you're in isn't punishment; it's **training**, *the normal experience of children. Only irresponsible parents leave children to fend for themselves. Would you prefer an irresponsible God? We respect our own parents for training and not spoiling us, so why not embrace God's training so we can truly* **live**?

HEBREWS 12:10-11

At times when I've lacked self-discipline, the lack has poured over into my discipline as a mother. I never want to be constantly on my children's case—and honestly, I've felt too exhausted to add disciplinarian to my list of things to do. However, when my oldest was three, I began to see the fruit born of a child raised without consistent discipline. Let me tell you, it wasn't sweet.

When children don't have consistent discipline, they indulge their feelings without regard to the consequences of their actions. Proverbs 22:15 says, "All children are foolish, but firm correction will make them change" (CEV). Discipline is all about forming character, shepherding a child to instill virtues like patience, forgiveness, work ethic, and responsibility. Adults with those character traits don't appear overnight; their characters are shaped and nurtured over time. So I began training my children more intentionally in order to raise disciplined adults.

God's discipline and process of sanctification—no matter how uncomfortable—reveals He loves us deeply and wants us to live out our purpose in

Him. He paid the ultimate price of His life in order for us to be in relationship with Him. We were too expensive for Him to allow us to act cheap and be immature disciples. Even as adults we are God's children, and because of sin, we can be foolish no matter our age. His correction is for our gain. He may allow difficulty in order to sanctify us. He may choose not to spare us from the consequences of our own choices. In whatever way God sanctifies and corrects, know that your endurance is creating a perfect result in you so "that you may be perfect and complete, lacking in nothing" (James 1:4 ESV).

READ

Job 5:17 ~ 2 Timothy 3:16-17

REFLECT

In what areas of your life do you lack discipline? Have you seen God's correction in those areas? Have you resisted God's loving correction, or have you been teachable?

PRAY WITH ME

Lord, soften my heart toward Your correction. Help me to be a fast learner. Thank You for loving me enough to show me the right and wrong ways to go. Give me endurance and steadfastness for the roads of correction that I will travel during my life in You.

REPENTANCE

God, God, a God of mercy and grace, endlessly patient—
so much love, so deeply true—loyal in love for a thousand
generations, forgiving iniquity, rebellion, and sin.

EXODUS 34:6-7

David had everything, yet his lust for a woman bathing on a roof still threw him off course. We've all been in a similar place, committed to following Christ yet seduced by distractions and ulterior motives. I've experienced the seduction of distractions at times with my health. When I've lost sight of obedience to God as my first priority, backsliding and vanity both swallowed me up. When we choose our lusts and fleshly desires over obedience to the Father, we quickly find that having what we want in the moment won't satiate us long.

But when David discovered his one-night stand would have a lasting effect in the form of Bathsheba's resulting pregnancy, he didn't seek repentance; instead, he covered up his wrongdoing by killing her husband. When the water is murky and we lose sight of obedience and commitment to God, we must repent. It took Nathan rebuking David for the king to finally see his sin and repent. Repentance requires more than remorse; it calls us to change our minds and reorient our way of thinking in order to forsake what is wrong. God told David that he would die for his actions, but because David acknowledged his sin, God lavished grace on him and saved his life. Still, a consequence for his action was the death of the child he fathered with Bathsheba. God doesn't spare us from every consequence of sin—a necessary lesson that can be hard for us to confront.

When we seek repentance, grace and mercy are available and accessible to anyone who asks for it. No matter the wrongdoing, if we move forward in obedience, even while suffering the consequences of our actions, God is good and rich in mercy toward us. Seek out an area in your life that is clouded by disobedience to His Word. Turn from your disobedience and acknowledge your sin. The Bible says in 2 Chronicles 7:14: "If my people who are called by my name humble themselves, and pray and seek my face and turn from their wicked ways, then I will hear from heaven and will forgive their sin and heal their land" (ESV). Repent, then you will see God's goodness more fully displayed in your life.

READ

Acts 3:19 ~ 2 Corinthians 7:10 ~ Revelation 2:5

REFLECT

Are you being seduced and distracted by the things of this world? What have been the natural consequences of your actions or lack of action? What would repentance look like for you? What do you need to turn from?

PRAY WITH ME

Father, illuminate the things I'm pursuing that are directly opposed to the things You've outlined in Your Word. Give me a renewed desire to please You instead of myself, and please place encouragers around me to remind me to endure in my ultimate goal: following Your will for my life.

WAITING FOR THE MOOD TO STRIKE

At the time, discipline isn't much fun. It always feels like it's going against the grain. Later, of course, it pays off big-time, for it's the well-trained who find themselves mature in their relationship with God.

HEBREWS 12:11

My sweet and only son, JT, is in the process of learning how to process his emotions. At times those feelings come out in a loud fit of anger or in a puddle of tears on the floor. When he quickly reacts to a negative situation, he can become fully overwhelmed by his emotions as they wash over him like a tidal wave. As a parent, it's heart-wrenching because I empathize with his emotions and his struggle to master them. However, it's my job to help him name his feelings and learn to communicate without allowing emotions to completely control him.

But I do feel his pain because focusing on feelings *feels* good. We have to be careful, however, to learn to name our emotions, communicate them, and then bring them to the throne of grace and under the authority of Christ. At times, our actions must take the driver's seat and drive our feelings instead of the other way around. Decisions can't be made from how we feel; instead, they must be measured against the truth of God's words and commands.

As someone who can be highly sensitive to feelings, many times I've been undisciplined. If I didn't *feel* like doing it, I didn't do it. This "feelings first" mentality was at the root of much of my underachievement. *Why can't I motivate myself toward action?* I used to ponder. Have you been there? Stuck waiting to feel energized and ready to accomplish, but doing nothing in the meanwhile because you're not in the mood? In order to achieve any goal, you have to overcome the lie that your feelings should dictate your every action. Feelings have the power to stand in the way of discipline.

God never asks us to feel a certain way in order to reach a goal. Instead, He simply commands obedience! It is imperative to trust God's command to obedience instead of the volatile nature of our emotions.

READ

2 Corinthians 10:5 ~ Galatians 5:16 ~ Proverbs 28:26

REFLECT

Put words to some of the feelings you have that keep you from action. Find at least two verses in the Bible for each feeling that holds you back, then commit the verses to memory.

PRAY WITH ME

Father, help me to prioritize my faith and actions over my feelings! Awaken the Holy Spirit in my heart to tell me the truth when my feelings try to run the show. I know You've given me feelings, and I thank You for them. But I know that allowing my emotions—rather than

Your commands—to dictate my life is a form of idolatry. I want to rid my heart of feelings that take precedence over truth. Speak to my heart through Christian friends, Your Word, and Your Spirit so I can understand my feelings within the light of Your truth.

GROWING WHERE PLANTED

Joseph replied, "Don't be afraid. Do I act for God? Don't you see, you planned evil against me but God used those same plans for my good, as you see all around you right now—life for many people."

GENESIS 50:19-20

I've always wanted a robust garden overflowing with crops and flowers. I even had an architect draw up plans for my dream garden and had big hopes for it to come to life. I refused to start smaller because I wanted that perfect greenhouse and readied garden before I began. But a few years later, with no garden built and no planted seeds, my mom bought me a countertop hydrogarden. It wasn't long after I had planted the tomatoes, basil, and thyme that came in the box that the plants were bursting out of the tabletop garden with growth, spilling onto the table, and yielding fruit. Because of the growth, we finally had a reason to begin garden construction so the plants grown had a place fit for their trajectory.

Many of us have big hopes and visions for the future of our lives in Christ. But like me with our garden, we like to go big or not at all. However, the beginning stages of growth into our purpose in Christ are crucial. Had I planted those tiny seedlings in the vast garden we had planned, they would have surely failed in the elements. The hydrogarden was the perfect safe place for the seedlings to blossom.

Joseph, sold by his brothers into slavery, was placed in low places after having big dreams. A servant and a prisoner who was eventually placed in charge of Egypt (Genesis 39–41), Joseph started from the bottom in unlikely and uncomfortable places while God prepared him for his ultimate position. While imprisoned, Joseph practiced interpreting the dreams of a cupbearer and a baker, and Joseph's wisdom and discernment in interpreting those dreams led to the king calling upon Joseph to interpret *his* dream. Then the king put Joseph in a role of authority over his palace and people (Genesis 41:39-40). But Joseph's journey began in prison—a place and time God used to train Joseph for a much greater purpose.

Right now, you also are being raised up in a place where God knows you can grow while He prepares what's next. Our Father does not give us more than we can bear, so take advantage of your circumstances and grow in the place He has set you. If you step out of God's place of preparation before your time, striving to reach a goal on your own, you can be easily swallowed up by the elements of a world you've not been spiritually prepared for. Embrace what God is doing now and be refined, filling up and overflowing with the love and knowledge He offers. His Holy Spirit is necessary for flourishing in the place He is preparing for you.

READ

1 Corinthians 7:17 ~ Isaiah 45:2 ~ 1 Chronicles 4:10

REFLECT

Where is God asking you to grow right now?
In what ways do you see opportunity for spiritual growth in the place where He has set you?

PRAY WITH ME

Father, instill in me patience to do what You are calling me to do now. Help me trust You with my future. Equip me in my current stage of life for the next one, and help me to be content in the place where You have me now. I put my trust in You and will not go before You but wait on Your divine timing for the dreams and vision You have for me. Give me discernment to know when You are calling me forward and when You are telling me to stay put.

COMPLETE SURRENDER

For whoever wants to save their life will lose it,
but whoever loses their life for me will save it.

LUKE 9:24 NIV

Our two-year-old, Josie, has been struggling to give up her bottle. For whatever reason, she keeps it by her side constantly and relies on it for comfort. Often, she doesn't even drink the milk but just holds the bottle nipple in her mouth. Recently, she was struggling to get up and into her brother's bunk bed. For me to lift her, I needed her to put both of her arms in the air so I could pick her up. But on this day, her arms were occupied as she held her bottle to her mouth. She screamed and cried because she needed help to get to the top of the bed, but she didn't want to relinquish the bottle in order to lift her hands in surrender.

For comparison, Scripture offers a perfect portrait of surrender in the life of Abraham. When God asks him to use his one and only, long awaited son, Isaac, as a sacrificial lamb, Genesis 22:3 says, "Abraham rose early in the morning, saddled his donkey, and took two of his young men with him, and his son Isaac. And he cut the wood for the burnt offering and arose and went to the place of which God had told him" (ESV). Abraham immediately obeyed, and as he took the knife to slaughter his son, an angel appeared with provisions for a new sacrifice so he did not have to lay a hand to Isaac.

There are so many things in this world to rightfully love. For Josie, it's her bottle, and for Abraham, his son. Many of the things we love and find comfort in have the potential to be so important to us that surrendering them to God proves difficult. This reminds me of a song that I recommend you go listen to called "He Wants It All" by Forever Jones.

So many times, I've asked God for help in different areas and heard, "I'm here. Lay this down so I can help you." And like Josie, I often haven't wanted to release my comforts and risk feeling hopeless and alone. Yet God was still there, waiting, ready to help when I released my crutches in exchange for His hand. Our Father in heaven asks us to completely surrender to Him and His will. That requires us to lay down what we treasure and hold dear in this world. It is important to note that when we actively lay down our worldly treasure, God is able to do exceedingly, abundantly more than what we'd hoped or imagined for in our surrender.

READ

Mark 8:34-35 ~ Ephesians 3:20 ~ Matthew 6:19-21

REFLECT

God asks that He be your help and that you be fully reliant and trusting of Him, so what do you need to lay down so you can hold on to Christ through your circumstances? What do you think would be the result if you surrendered to God? If you're struggling to trust Him, what can you actively do to restore trust and surrender in your relationship with Christ?

PRAY WITH ME

Father, I know that surrendering my earthly treasure is directly related to the trust I have in You. Lead me graciously as I surrender my will and my treasures to You in complete faith. If there is any distrust in my heart, please soothe my soul. Give me peace and ease my fear with Your loving-kindness as I hand over every part of my life.

PAIN OVER PLEASURE

I quit focusing on the handicap and began appreciating the gift. It was a case of Christ's strength moving in on my weakness. Now I take limitations in stride, and with good cheer, these limitations that cut me down to size—abuse, accidents, opposition, bad breaks. I just let Christ take over! And so the weaker I get, the stronger I become.

2 CORINTHIANS 12:10

I stared into the gym mirror on leg day, focused on perfect form as I squatted repetitively with a heavy weight on my shoulders. My legs were trembling and achy; the pain was almost intolerable. In my previous attempts at going to the gym, I could barely make it through a set. Fixated on the pain, I'd cop out early, convincing myself I couldn't do any more. But this time was different. I wasn't concentrating on the aches shooting through my legs. Instead, my mind was set on the vision God gave me for my health as it relates to my purpose. There was no room in my mind for the pain at hand. I could clearly picture my goal of having more energy to play with my babies, a better work ethic, and stronger discipline in all areas of my life. I left no space for dwelling on short-lived pain.

When God calls you toward a goal, choose to focus on the purpose God can achieve through you instead of fixating on the momentary displeasure. With Christ as your focus, you can wrestle with intention through difficult circumstances, knowing you don't wrestle for worldly gain but eternal. Through trial, you are being strengthened in your faith. The Bible says in

Ephesians 6:12, "We do not wrestle against flesh and blood, but against the rulers, against the authorities, against the cosmic powers over this present darkness, against the spiritual forces of evil in the heavenly places" (ESV).

A spiritual battle can even look like a physical one. In Matthew 17:14-20, a boy's father kneels before Jesus. The man asks for Him to have mercy on his son, who has seizures causing him to fall into fire and water. This boy was on the losing side of a battle with spiritual forces of evil in heavenly places, because in response to his physical ailment, Jesus rebukes a demon and the boy is healed instantly. In order to withstand trials both spiritual and physical in nature, we must be strengthened spiritually through trial and still "press on toward the goal for the prize of the upward call of God in Christ Jesus" (Philippians 3:14 ESV).

Set your mind on Christ as you are stretched and being made new. Do not be distracted, discouraged, or disillusioned by the spiritual and even physical discomfort you may feel along the journey of spiritual maturation. Set your mind on God's vision for your life, and recognize that pain in this life is temporary. Christ "will transform our lowly body to be like his glorious body" (Philippians 3:21 ESV)!

READ

2 Corinthians 12:7-10 ~ Psalm 119:71

REFLECT

Like Paul's "thorn," what trials, big or small, are you enduring in your life right now? How can you see God using these thorns, when given to Him, to foster spiritual maturity in your life? What are ways you can alter your mindset to focus on having faith?

PRAY WITH ME

Father, You used Jesus's pain, suffering, and death—the most horrific and unjust trial ever endured—to redeem humanity. I know Your power is made perfect in weakness and that You transform hardship for Your glory! I desire to see that in my own life. Give me a renewed mind as I fixate on You in the face of my own weakness. If it is Your will, let me witness how You're using my current suffering to advance Your kingdom. But if I cannot know or see that yet, uplift my spirit with the knowledge that even my darkest, weakest moments allow Your goodness and strength to be known.

SPIRITUAL DIETS

Don't look for shortcuts to God. The market is flooded with surefire, easygoing formulas for a successful life that can be practiced in your spare time. Don't fall for that stuff, even though crowds of people do. The way to life—to God!—is vigorous and requires total attention.

MATTHEW 7:13-14

I've spent much of my adult life after birthing children trying out weight-loss plans only to realize there is no quick path to success. Whether it's a low-carb diet or a juice cleanse, these so-called shortcuts might give me a small amount of short-term success, but I haven't found one that helps me with sustainable weight loss, let alone with building a healthy relationship with food and body image. Yet despite knowing these magic-bullet weight-loss plans won't work, what they falsely offer is still so appealing that I—and millions of others—are still willing to give them a try. Committing to changing how we approach and consume food, building regular exercise into our busy lives, and even improving our self-image might be the best way to get healthier and find peace with our bodies, but that's a lot of work for results that might take a while to see. We cling to the hope that somewhere an easy-to-follow formula exists for quickly getting the body of our dreams.

Like my search for a magic-bullet weight-loss plan, I've also gone on spiritual quick-fix "diets." When I had a problem that was beyond me, I'd approach my faith like it was a new workout regimen: praying consistently, reading my Bible, and begging God for my problem to be solved. Just like a weight-loss plan, I was motivated by the hope of fast results gained by new habits that would probably be dropped as soon as my goals were met.

Spiritual growth doesn't work like that. God is not a genie in a bottle who can be summoned to fix our problems and then dismissed once we feel better. He wants to be the center point around which our lives revolve. He wants a faith from us that is active and always growing, developed through trust, prayer, and time in His Word. He longs to be in a loving relationship with His followers—but He is not in our lives simply so we can take advantage of His power. Colossians 1:17 tells us: "He is before all things, and in him all things hold together" (ESV). His presence in our lives is a privilege, and to truly experience the fruits of faith, we must be invested in God Himself and not the perks we think should come with being a Christian.

For physical health, lasting change only happens with a wholehearted and long-term commitment. For spiritual health, walking alongside the Father takes your wholehearted attention. God deserves and requires as much, and pursuing faith is the ultimate lifestyle change that will completely engulf our hearts and minds. But when we are living in commitment to Him, we find peace and joy beyond what we could ever imagine finding on our own.

READ

1 Kings 8:61 ~ Jeremiah 29:13 ~ 2 Chronicles 16:9

REFLECT

Are you guilty of going on spiritual diets to solve the problems at hand instead of opting for a long-term commitment to God? What do you want from your faith?

PRAY WITH ME

I want my relationship with You, Father, to be long-lasting. I don't want a fad prayer life or to only come to You when there's a problem. Ignite a fire in me, and give me the overwhelming desire to pursue You daily.

PART SIX

JESUS DRAWS US CLOSE

BLESSED PERSISTENCE

May the Lord repay you for what you have done. May you be richly rewarded by the Lord, the God of Israel, under whose wings you have come to take refuge.

RUTH 2:12 NIV

In Ruth 2:6-9, we see Ruth working tirelessly to pick up fallen grain behind the laborers of a field. A Moabite woman widowed by a Jewish man, Ruth made the countercultural decision to remain a part of her Jewish community after her husband's death so she could support her mother-in-law, Naomi. She also chose to continue worshiping Yahweh, the God who had once been foreign to her. With no means to support Naomi and herself, Ruth took to gathering in the fields, working so hard that she caught the attention of Boaz, the field's owner and Ruth's future husband. "'Who is this young woman? Where did she come from?'" he asked the field's overseer, who told Boaz of Ruth's commendable work ethic (Ruth 2:5-7). What did Boaz do at the mention of her hard work? He commanded his servants to pull extra stalks to leave for her to pick up (Ruth 2:16). Because she was so committed and persistent, she was blessed; not only was she able to gather more grain, but she earned Boaz's respect through her hard work. After Boaz married her, Ruth went on to become the great-grandmother of King David, and now she's one of the five women named in the bloodline of Christ (Matthew 1:4).

For us today, Ruth is a model of both praiseworthy persistence and of

God's promise to reward those who are faithful to Him. Ruth's hard work and loyalty to her faith and family were independent of her eventual reward; she didn't know when she chose to remain with Naomi or when she worked tirelessly each day that God had so many bigger and better things in store for her. Further, we don't know if Ruth knew the full extent to which God rewarded her; the Bible doesn't indicate that she knew she would become the great-grandmother of Israel's future king or in the bloodline of mankind's eternal Savior. But she didn't need to know the details of what God had in store to know He was worthy of her faithfulness.

This is the responsive attitude that we, as Christians, should model in our lives today. Even when we do not know what God has in store, and even when we cannot see the ways in which He will pay our inheritance in full, we can still choose to work with joy and diligence, trusting in God always.

Be committed, be persistent, and be faithful to God with your work, knowing that He will reward your faithfulness.

READ

Ruth 1:16-17 ~ Psalm 51:17

REFLECT

In the small tasks and mundane work of your daily life, how is God calling you to worship Him? How can you respond in faithfulness and persistence, as Ruth did? Is anything holding you back from trusting that He has what is best for you in store?

PRAY WITH ME

Dear God, throughout the Bible, we see Your incredible work and kindness in the lives of those who follow You. Even when I am unsure where You are leading me, please help me follow with an open heart, ready to journey in faith down whatever path You have before me.

BREATH

We take our lead from Christ, who is the source of everything we do. He keeps us in step with each other. His very breath and blood flow through us, nourishing us so that we will grow up healthy in God, robust in love.

EPHESIANS 4:15-16

When JT was born, he didn't breathe for a minute and a half. After six hours of labor, seeing my baby lying on my chest looking limp and lifeless filled me with bone-chilling dread. Those 90 seconds felt longer than the hours it had taken to push him out. For a minute and a half, my midwives gave him CPR while my aunt blanketed us in prayer. Finally, he inhaled—and so did I. My midwives explained later that they left the baby connected to the umbilical cord during CPR, because as long as the cord was connecting us, oxygen was flowing through me to his brain and body. Although his lungs needed to breathe on their own, he was still safe as long as he was connected to his life-giving source.

Just as newborns are dependent on and connected to their mothers, we are also safe when connected to *the* life-giving Source. In times when we feel suffocated by worries about the future, we can find comfort knowing that God pumps life into us when we are connected to Him, no matter the circumstance. When the news reports a tragedy, we can take comfort by remembering that Christ will come again in glory and wipe away our every tear (Revelation 21:4). When we struggle with indecision or uncertainty, we can find hope in the knowledge that God doesn't change and knows all the days of our lives (Psalm 139:18). When we're tempted toward selfishness or unkindness, we can invite God to show His love to others through us. A Christ-centered life in which we are connected to the Father through an active relationship gives us peace. Instead of fighting on our own, we have been promised that the battle is already won.

READ

Exodus 14:13-14 ~ Revelation 21:4 ~ Psalm 46:1

REFLECT

Consider a past hardship where you felt scared or overwhelmed, yet you realized on the other side that God took care of you through your trial. What lessons about God's provision can you take from this experience and remember for the future?

PRAY WITH ME

Lord, thank You for being the ultimate lifeline! When life leaves me floundering and gasping for air, please remind me to cling to You—knowing that I am secure, knowing that You uphold me with Your righteous right hand.

WAKE UP

Wake up from your sleep,
Climb out of your coffins;
Christ will show you the light!

EPHESIANS 5:14

In my midtwenties, a shift occurred in my walk with Jesus. The result of that shift was an inability to keep Jesus to myself. To not bring Him up in conversation was nearly impossible, and I delighted in hearing what other people were learning about Him in their own lives. My brother noticed this shift and blurted out one day, "When did you get so spiritual?!" For the first time, I was able to trace my newly found love for Christ back to the death of my cousin Wynter, who died suddenly at age 38. She left behind her husband, Jonathan, and their four young daughters—yet incredibly, Jonathan continued to worship and praise God amid this life-changing tragedy. I told my brother that witnessing her sudden passing and Jonathan's faith-filled response not only helped me understand Christ's comfort in times of grief but also helped me realize that this life isn't what we live for.

When God said this life is like a vapor, a breath, or a passing shadow, He meant it (Psalm 144:4). We will spend endless ages with Him in eternity, walking by sight instead of by faith—but right now, this life is an invitation to show our total devotion to Him. We are His creatures, and we were created to be loved by Him and to love Him in return. We weren't created to live selfishly. We were made to be living arrows—to use the talents, gifts, and abilities He's given us to point directly back to Him and His goodness.

The goal of this life is to someday hear God say, "Well done, good and faithful servant" (Matthew 25:21 NIV). Will you hear that in the end? Do you want there to be a question, or do you want to doubt that God was your number-one priority while you were here on earth? When I shared this conviction with my brother, he simply nodded his head at my explanation, as may you. But will you take it to heart and get serious about living your life solely for the Father?

As a mother of small children, let me tell you: Kids have little to no concept of time. Days, weeks, months, and years mean nothing to them. Small children wake up every day searching for enjoyment and living for fun. There is a time for childhood. However, as adults, we can't afford to be spiritual children. Living unaware of time while searching only for enjoyment risks our eternity.

Up until July 21, 2018, I had been spiritually childish, living incognizant of wasted time. Then, Wynter woke me up with her God-centered, purpose-filled life and incredible legacy. If you have been wasting your unpromised time living for personal gratification, wake up! Every day God gives you is an opportunity to show that you are indeed His good and faithful servant. Let's live fully today, tomorrow, and beyond by intentionally focusing on the purpose God has set before us and pursuing it with our whole hearts.

READ

1 Corinthians 15:58 ~ Colossians 3:23-24 ~ Revelation 3:11

REFLECT

God wants hearing "Well done, good and faithful servant" to be your heart's greatest priority. Does your life reflect this? This week, what's one small change you can make to help you better focus on this ultimate goal of serving God?

PRAY WITH ME

Lord, Your Word and the sacrifice of Your only Son have changed our lives forever. I choose to not take that lightly and to live my life differently so You would receive the glory! I know this life on earth isn't the end, so today, help me live with Your boldness and courage. Show me how to live in Your reality even while I'm awaiting eternity with You.

NOT FULLY FUNCTIONAL

When you're joined with me and I with you, the relation is intimate and organic, the harvest is sure to be abundant. Separated, you can't produce a thing.

JOHN 15:5

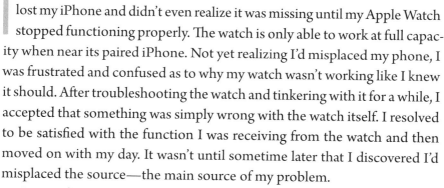

I lost my iPhone and didn't even realize it was missing until my Apple Watch stopped functioning properly. The watch is only able to work at full capacity when near its paired iPhone. Not yet realizing I'd misplaced my phone, I was frustrated and confused as to why my watch wasn't working like I knew it should. After troubleshooting the watch and tinkering with it for a while, I accepted that something was simply wrong with the watch itself. I resolved to be satisfied with the function I was receiving from the watch and then moved on with my day. It wasn't until sometime later that I discovered I'd misplaced the source—the main source of my problem.

Many of us aren't functioning at our full capacity because we aren't joined or connected to *our* Source. We were made in the image of God, so when distanced from the original image, we can't access the power available to us. We may even resolve to be satisfied with what we can get, settling for "good enough" even though God has so much more in store.

It is impossible to grow when we are not connected to Christ. While writing this devotional, I experienced lulls in my ability to write simply because I was not staying connected to the vine that is Christ (John 15:1).

Our purpose in Him is hindered when we aren't intentional about joining ourselves to Him, yet without Him, nothing is worth doing. All things were made through Him, so how can we expect to thrive when we're disconnected? (John 1:3).

READ

1 Corinthians 15:58 ~ Colossians 3:23-24 ~ Revelation 3:11

REFLECT

In seasons when you haven't been intentional about pursuing Christ, what was the fruit of your disconnection? What signs in your life—attitudes, actions, or struggles—reminded you of your deep need for closeness with Him? Today, what steps can you take to either maintain or reestablish your connection?

PRAY WITH ME

I want to be close and connected with You as my Source, Father. Make evident the areas of my life where I've disconnected from You and have lived half-full. I want to live fully in Your will, and I know that to do so I must be close to You. Show me what I must remove from or add to my life in order to gain proximity to You.

COMPROMISE

Some of you wandered for years in the desert, looking but not finding a good place to live, Half-starved and parched with thirst, staggering and stumbling, on the brink of exhaustion. Then, in your desperate condition, you called out to God. He got you out in the nick of time; He put your feet on a wonderful road that took you straight to a good place to live.

PSALM 107:4-7

After losing a considerable amount of weight, I thought about things I'd given up for the momentary satisfaction of food. I'd given up my health, clothes I loved wearing, energy for my kids, and more, all for French fries and Cokes on a regular basis. When I was hungry (and even when I wasn't), finding my next food fix could feel like a life-and-death situation. I traded time God destined for growth for a meal. Every time I made a poor choice because food was my master, I disqualified myself from the blessing of honoring God with a body wholly given to Him.

Long ago, Esau gave away his birthright for a bowl of soup. We've heard the story a hundred times, but does that not still sound ridiculously silly? He handed over his inheritance of a double share of his father's estate so he could satisfy a temporary hunger (Deuteronomy 21:17). He said, "I am about to die" (Genesis 25:32 ESV), but I find it hard to believe that missing one meal would have ended his life right then and there. Yet Esau's momentary desperation compelled him to trade a lifetime of blessing for short-term satisfaction.

When we feel we are starving, we compromise in ways we never thought we would. When you feel starved of love, do you give yourself away physically? When you feel starved of acceptance, do you compromise your faith to fit in? Looking back on your own life, what have you given up because you felt "starved"? Is that a sacrifice you're still making right now?

Today, choose to submit your desires wholly to Christ and see how He satisfies your heart's deepest hunger. Don't trade in your blessings for short-lived satisfaction. Remember Psalm 107:9: "He poured great drafts of water down parched throats; the starved and hungry got plenty to eat."

READ

Acts 17:27 ~ James 4:8 ~ 1 Peter 2:4-5

REFLECT

What are you hungry for? What placeholders in your life do you run to when your heart is truly hungry for Christ and the fullness of life He brings? Create a practice you can implement to help you turn to Christ when you feel tempted to seek a placeholder for His presence.

PRAY WITH ME

There's no one above You, Father. I know any attempt I've made at filling my own void has been in vain. You are the only One who can make my life full. You are the well that will never run dry. Equip me with Your Word to fend off the enemy's attempts to derail my life with idols. Open my eyes to see what I've put before You. Give me the desire to put aside all other masters. You bring life and more life, and I long to serve You alone.

CHOOSING OBEDIENCE

Your lives must be totally obedient to God, our personal God, following the life path he has cleared, alert and attentive to everything he has made plain this day.

1 KINGS 8:61

While we were getting dressed for Easter, I asked my daughter to bring me her sparkly Sunday shoes. These specific instructions should have elicited an immediate and obedient reaction. But within a few minutes, I could hear loud clunking coming down the hallway. The heavy steps didn't sound like the shoes I'd asked for. Instead of her Sunday shoes, she proudly kicked out her foot to display her white lace boots. "Mommy! *These* are the shoes I want!" she said.

I responded, "Yes, but those aren't the shoes I asked you to get. Try again." On the second and third trips, she showed me her silver Velcro sneakers and then her pink swimming shoes. Although nice shoes, none were what I'd asked from her. In the end, my daughter's effort and time was wasted; she still had to go back and choose obedience.

We all know when God is asking something specific of us. He is clear in His Word, and He is clear when He calls us to action through the power of the Holy Spirit. Often, we are willing to give Him everything *but* what He's asking of us. But in the Bible, we see God praising those who respond faithfully in perfect obedience. When God asked Abraham to sacrifice his only son, Isaac, Abraham didn't say, "You know what, God, how about this lamb instead?" Rather, Genesis 22:3 says, "Abraham got up early in the morning and saddled his donkey." He obeyed immediately, bringing Isaac with him on a journey to a sacrificial altar. But once he had bound and prepared Isaac, ready to follow God's commands, God called him to stop and provided him with a ram to take Isaac's place. God spared Isaac's life and praised Abraham's obedience: "Now I know how fearlessly you fear God" (Genesis 22:12).

God never asked me to sacrifice my child, but He has asked for a lot of things I wasn't ready to give. I'll be the first to admit I've "obeyed" the way my daughter tried to, offering everything except what God asked of me. Together, let's practice giving what God asks of us, knowing His promises are true and He will always come through.

READ

1 John 5:14-15 ~ Joshua 1:8 ~ Deuteronomy 11:27

REFLECT

Are there any compromises or half measures you're taking in your faith to try to appease both God and yourself? Knowing that God commands full obedience, ask Him to move you to complete submission. If these compromises have become habits, giving them up may be more of a process than a one-and-done decision. If this is the case for you, consider how you can make a long-term plan for building new habits that will allow you to be faithful to what God is asking of you.

PRAY WITH ME

Lord, I want to be the kind of follower who will put everything on the altar for You. Thank You for Your grace when I fall short. Thank You for allowing me to return to You and welcoming me with love when I am disobedient, but don't allow me to be comfortable with where I am. Please convict me in the areas where I am making compromises, and please help me surrender fully to You—giving You what You desire from me every day and standing strong against the temptation to settle for a "close enough" kind of faithfulness.

A GUIDING HAND

Your teacher will be right there, local and on the job, urging you on whenever you wander left or right: "This is the right road. Walk down this road."

ISAIAH 30:21

In between large cities in Texas lies the mother of all rest stops: Buc-ee's. We usually stop at the Buc-ee's between Houston and Dallas during our back-and-forth trips for work. The last time we made our usual stop was on a Saturday, and Buc-ee's was popping. Seeing the maze of people we had to make our way through, I placed my hand on my daughter's shoulder as a steering wheel through the crowd she couldn't see over.

When Ellie was distracted by candy, chips, or a toy, she would pull away in another direction. But the more she tried to venture off, the firmer my hand steered and corrected her. Guidance was more difficult when she thought she knew enough to go her own way, and it was easier for her to go where I was guiding her than to struggle against me. Not only did I know what and who was coming at us, but I also knew which route was safe and would benefit us the most.

As the ultimate wise and loving parent, God has His gentle hand placed firmly on the shoulders of His children. He has a better view and knows infinitely more than we think we do, and it's easier for us to lean into His direction than resist His mindful guidance. When we feel resistance in our attempts to follow and nothing seems to be going the way we planned, we have to stop and ask ourselves if it's because we're fighting against God's firm-but-gentle hand on our lives.

At times it may be uncomfortable to let Jesus sit in the driver's seat, since many of us think we know best. But resisting only causes us more pain, struggle, and time, and combating His direction will surely lead us down the wrong road. Meanwhile, the result of following His direction is receiving the guidance of a Father who knows the past, present, and future—a God who sees all there is to be seen, including all we cannot see. Trusting His hand to lead us in the way we should go leads us to life more abundant.

READ

Acts 7:51 ~ Isaiah 48:17 ~ Psalm 32:8

REFLECT

When have you experienced tension in your life caused by resisting the hand of God upon your shoulders? What did it look like when you stopped tugging and instead leaned into His direction? When you allowed yourself to be guided by God's will, what fruits came with obedience? How does this firsthand knowledge encourage you to submit today?

PRAY WITH ME

Lord, I don't know how to lead myself through this life, even and especially when I'm confident that I do. Please make me willing and ready to accept Your direction and walk upon whatever path You've set for me. Help me submit to You and the direction You have planned for me.

SEPARATION ANXIETY

You're all I want in heaven! You're all I want on earth! When my skin sags and my bones get brittle, God is rock-firm and faithful.

PSALM 73:25-26

My husband and I are always together. And when I say "always," I mean it. We live together, work together, relax together, fight it out together, and raise kids together. Very rarely are we apart for more than a few hours at a time. So when my husband took a trip with my grandfather recently, I experienced a shocking amount of separation anxiety. Like a kid away from their family for the first time at camp, I was a ball of tears every night. I used to cherish my alone time, but now, time without him feels empty. When you are often in close proximity to someone, time apart is felt deeply.

Marriage reflects Christ's relationship with us, the church. Even more than a relationship with a spouse, our bond with God is so intimate, so closely knit, that the moment we take our eyes off Him, we're lost, confused, purposeless. The discomfort and even pain that result from taking our eyes off Christ should remind us to return to our life-giving relationship with our Savior and Creator.

Don't become desensitized to the absence of your heavenly Father in your daily life. Are you so close to God that you experience separation anxiety the minute you step out of alignment with Him? Strive to stay so connected to Him that even a short departure from Him catapults you back into

His loving arms. And as you rest there, remember that even if you took your eyes off God, he *never* removed His gaze from you. As Romans 8:39 puts it, "Absolutely *nothing* can get between us and God's love because of the way that Jesus our Master has embraced us."

READ

1 Peter 2:2 ~ Psalm 51:10

REFLECT

Think about the last time you ventured away from God. What reminded you to return to your relationship with Him? Have you ever become desensitized to His absence in your life? What can you do to form a more consistent relationship with God?

PRAY WITH ME

Father, I want to be near You and be so sensitive to Your presence that I'm keenly aware when I'm no longer in it. Hide Your Word in my heart, and empower the Holy Spirit to bring it to the forefront of my mind daily so I may stay in constant fellowship with You.

STAY CLOSE

Be very careful to act exactly as God commands you. Don't veer off to the right or the left. Walk straight down the road God commands so that you'll have a good life and live a long time in the land that you're about to possess.

DEUTERONOMY 5:32-33

One rainy morning while getting Ellie ready for school, I bundled her up in her lime green froggy rain jacket and sent her out the door with Josh, who was waiting with a dad-sized umbrella to usher her safely from the garage to the car. He gave her the instruction, "Stay close to Daddy so you don't get wet." But she got sidetracked by the mud puddles and strayed behind. When she got soaked and began to cry, Josh went back to her with the umbrella. Gently, he reminded her that if she'd been intentional in her obedience and stayed close to Daddy, she would have remained safe and dry.

Similarly, God gave His people clear instructions as they formed a new nation and made their way to the Promised Land. These laws were for their protection; when followed, the instructions would ensure that God's people thrived in the land He had set apart for them. Yet the Israelites got sidetracked along the way, creating a harmful pattern of disobedience. They lacked faith before crossing the Red Sea (Exodus 14:10). They complained over the bitter water at Marah (Exodus 15:22-27). They kept manna when told not to (Exodus 16:19-20). They engaged in idolatry (Exodus 32). As a result of disobeying God time and time again, the Israelites' journey to the Promised Land was sidetracked, and they wandered the desert for 40 years.

Obedience keeps us not only close to the God who knows His purpose for us, but safe under the cover of His protection. It is in our own best interests to follow Him without doubting His direction, complaining about our circumstances, or greedily desiring more than He has given us. Like the Israelites, we will find ourselves circling a wilderness of our own making, delaying the safety and good gifts our Father has set aside. Be obedient and see how the Father covers you, even in the rain.

READ

Psalm 91:4 ~ Deuteronomy 4:1-2 ~ Psalm 119:33-35

REFLECT

What distracts you from remaining obedient to your heavenly Father? What reminders or calls to obedience might He be giving you that you're either ignoring or overlooking? What actions can you take to better focus on His instructions for you?

PRAY WITH ME

Father, thank You for offering Your protection and guidance to me, a sinner. I am blessed to receive Your covering. Give me the wisdom to identify distractions in my life so I can see them for what they are. Help keep my eyes trained on You, and may my actions stay in line with the obedience You call me toward.

SHIFTING FOCUS

You'll do best by filling your minds and meditating on things true, noble, reputable, authentic, compelling, gracious... Put into practice what you learned from me, what you heard and saw and realized. Do that, and God, who makes everything work together, will work you into his most excellent harmonies.

PHILIPPIANS 4:8-9

Ellie went through a phase in which she did not want to leave places that were fun-filled. If we were ready to leave somewhere and she was still having a ball, she would lose it—the screaming-on-the-floor, everything-is-a-problem, inconsolable type of losing it. But during the times when she was mid-breakdown, instead of disciplining her, I'd talk her off the ledge by shifting her focus. I'd command her attention and say, "Ellie! Did you have fun playing with your cousins? Wasn't your dinner delicious? Jumping on the trampoline seemed fun!" While I reviewed the good things and asked her to talk about them with me, I could always see her face change as she focused her mind on what was good. Now as a seven-year-old, I see her putting this into practice on her own as she has learned to set her mind on what is good.

You may not be having three-year-old-Ellie-sized fits, but perhaps you grumble on your way to work, tap your feet with impatience in the checkout line, or take out your frustrations on those you love most. Like Ellie, many of us need to shift our focus. We concentrate on the negative and complain, missing the reality of the many blessings God has already given us.

As you go about the details of your day, consider what you can praise God for. Are you fed? Do you have the luxury of sleeping in a bed at night? Was there a job waiting for you when you woke up this morning? Were you given a new day to make the most of? Does God use the parts of your day that are hard, bad, or tedious to help you grow in faith? Adopt an attitude of thankfulness and watch how that gratitude transforms you.

READ

Numbers 11:1 ~ Jude 1:15 ~ Philippians 2:14-15

REFLECT

What situations most often lead you to grumble and complain? List a few—then find ways in each of them to count it all joy and offer God praise.

PRAY WITH ME

Heavenly Father, equip me to change my perspective on my circumstances so I can be grateful for things I've not been thankful for. Open my eyes to see the good that surrounds me.
Give me a new perspective and outlook on my life.

IN THE SAFEST HANDS

His huge outstretched arms protect you—
under them you're perfectly safe; his arms fend off all harm.

PSALM 91:4

The first few times we took Ellie skating, she would burst into loud and uncontrollable laughter anytime she tripped or fell. At first I was baffled as to why falling was amusing to her, but I slowly realized that because either Josh or I was there holding her hand, her falls were never as hard as they would have been if she were on her own. Though we sometimes allowed her to fall with the intention of teaching her how to skate, those stumbles were softened because we held her hand. She knew she wasn't in any danger of being hurt even when she fell, so she laughed, ready to be helped back up for her next attempt.

Just like us as parents, our heavenly Father allows us to fall at times in order to teach us. However, we don't stumble and suffer the consequences of our sins in isolation. He is present with us and often softens the blow. We can take heart in the failing and in the learning, thanking Him for cushioning the bump and picking us back up again.

Whenever we are onboarding a new team member into our business, the first system we teach them is one that helps with organization. The system we created inside of this application has many checklists to help the new team member know the next step as they grasp their new position. In times when they miss a step or forget what comes next in their workflow, they know they can go back to the organization application, find stability, and continue their good work.

Our Father knows we will fail; it is the curse of Adam for us to do so. But His hand is mighty enough to save us and put us back on our feet so we can try again. We should look to Christ—our wonderful, omnipotent counselor—as our help in times of trouble, because with God on our side, we cannot fail. We are empowered to push on, no matter how many times we have to rise again. As children of the most high God, we live in the knowledge that we have a purpose to accomplish before He calls us home.

READ

Romans 8:28 ~ 2 Corinthians 12:9-10 ~ Psalm 16:11

REFLECT

How do you choose to look at your failures? Do you allow them to devastate you, or do you thank God for the learning experience? In what ways can you find joy amid life's tumbles?

PRAY WITH ME

Lord, thank You for softening the blow when I fall, and thank You for always picking me back up again. I'm sorry if I've ever looked at my stumbles as anything other than learning experiences. I always want You to be right beside me, cheering me on as I go through life. Thank You for never leaving.

A PLACE FOR YOU

If someone has a hundred sheep and one of them wanders off, doesn't he leave the ninety-nine and go after the one? And if he finds it, doesn't he make far more over it than over the ninety-nine who stay put? Your Father in heaven feels the same way. He doesn't want to lose even one of these simple believers.

MATTHEW 18:12-14

A few days ago, while walking into—you'll never guess—Chick-fil-A, I walked past a rugged young man. He wasn't asking for anything, so we smiled at each other, and I kept my eye on the prize. But while in line for my golden fries, I couldn't stop thinking about him. *What was his story? Was he homeless? Why was he standing there, not asking for anything?* I shook off my questions and ordered.

On my way out, we exchanged smiles again, and I began a race-walk to my car. (Those hot fries were screaming my name.) But halfway there, I felt a still small voice stopping me in the middle of the street. *"You say you want Me to use you, but you're choosing hot fries over loving one of Mine?"*

"But Lord! My hot fries!" I argued.

"But that's one of my sons," I heard.

Begrudgingly, I turned around, trying not to think about my fries, which were getting colder by the second.

"Are you hungry?" I asked the man.

"Yes, ma'am," he replied.

"All right, then," I said. "Let's get you fed."

Once we were inside the restaurant, I asked him to tell me about himself. The line was long, so we had a few minutes together for me to learn that he was living in a shelter. His father lived nearby, and he wanted his son to come home.

I wasn't pulling punches at this point, so I asked, lovingly, "Why in the world are you living at a shelter if your dad wants you to come home?"

He shrugged. "I guess I just want to be independent."

I laughed a little bit. "How's that working out for you?"

He laughed too. "I guess not too good, huh?"

Before I could even think, my mouth flew open and said, "Boy, if you don't *go home*!" He had a dad who loved him and had offered him a place. However, this man's desire to do things his own way kept him from warmth, safety, and shelter.

We are all unsuccessfully independent without our heavenly Father. He calls to us saying, "Come home! I have a place for you." But many of us call back, "I'd rather be free and independent!" What we often miss is that when it comes to our hearts, independence doesn't equal victory!

After purchasing his meal, I put a hand on his shoulder. "God loves you. He wants you home just like your dad does, and today He wanted to make sure you had a meal."

When I got back to my car, I ate the best cold fries I've ever had.

READ

1 Timothy 6:6 ~ Isaiah 58:11 ~ Psalm 73:25-26

REFLECT

As Christians, we may *know* that the best place is in God's house, but like the prodigal son, we may still fall into the trap of *feeling* like we'd have more fun on our own. What biblical truths counter the temptations that make your heart prone to straying? How can you find the satisfaction you're looking for within your Father's loving arms?

PRAY WITH ME

Lord, I may be tempted to consider what life would look like on my own, and I may even have fallen into the trap of pursuing this false freedom. I know what I could gain through my own strength would never come close to the rich inheritance I already have in You. I want to repent of my shortsightedness and let my wandering heart find its home in You. Thank You for always welcoming me home with open arms, no matter how long I've been away.

ACKNOWLEDGMENTS

First and foremost, thank you to my husband, Joshua. You listened to me and heard me when I said I wanted to write and consistently made space for me to do what I love by providing in abundance for our home and our family. You've yet to stop encouraging me. Your positivity, love, and support are the reasons I didn't quit on this book. This is as much yours as it is mine. Thank you, thank you, thank you.

Lois Elizabeth, Joshua Thomas II, Josephine Grace, and Evelyn Roxana, you four munchkins both inspired this devotional and kept me from writing it. I dreamt about and prayed for each one of you since I was 13, but I couldn't have imagined how Jesus would show me so clearly who He is through you. Thank you for being the lights of my life and bringing me so much joy.

To Poppy, we both know you "got me this job"! Thank you to both you and Nonny for your never-ending, unwavering love and support. You have always been my immovable, solid foundation. Thank you for fathering me through every season of my life.

To Auntie Silla, when I have felt unsure or been too hard on myself in any area of my life, you have been my cheerleader. You helped give me the confidence that I could write a book. When I would get overwhelmed and stressed during the writing process, your advice consistently got me over the hump. Thank you for being my friend who gives wise and absolutely hilarious encouragement and counsel.

To my first editor at Harvest House, Kathleen Kerr, thank you for diving into this book with me. You edited this book in a way that further brought Jesus into the spotlight. You helped better center my stories around the One who is, and is to come. You understood the assignment, girl. Thank you.

To Bob Hawkins, Sherrie Slopianka, and the team at Harvest House Publishers, thank you for sitting down with me and listening to the heart behind this devotional before it came to be. The guidance, support, and genuine care from you both and the whole team at Harvest House made writing this book with Harvest House an immense pleasure. Thank you.

EVERYWHERE-JESUS EVE
HERE-JESUS EVERYWHER
SUS EVERYWHERE-JESUS
RYWHERE-JESUS EVERYW
RE-JESUS EVERYWHERE-J
VERYWHERE-JESUS EVER
WHERE-JESUS EVERYWHE
-JESUS EVERYWHERE-JES
VERYWHERE-JESUS EVER
RYWHERE-JESUS EVERY
HERE-JESUS EVERYWHER
SUS EVERYWHERE-JESUS
VERYWHERE-JESUS EVER
HERE-JESUS EVERYWHER
VERYWHERE-JESUS EVE

ESUS EVERYWHERE-JESUS
ERYWHERE-JESUS EVERY
ERE-JESUS EVERYWHERE
US EVERYWHERE-JESUS E
YWHERE-JESUS EVERYWH
ESUS EVERYWHERE-JESU
EVERYWHERE-JESUS EVE
WHERE-JESUS EVERYWH
ESUS EVERYWHERE-JESU
US EVERYWHERE-JESUS
VERYWHERE-JESUS EVER
ERE-JESUS EVERYWHER
ESUS EVERYWHERE-JESUS
ERYWHERE-JESUS EVERY
ESUS EVERYWHERE-JESU